# MONARCHY

## The History of an Idea

### BRENDA RALPH LEWIS

SUTTON PUBLISHING

First published in the United Kingdom in 2003 by
Sutton Publishing Limited · Phoenix Mill
Thrupp · Stroud · Gloucestershire · GL5 2BU

British Library Cataloguing in Publication Data
A catalogue record for this book is available from the British Library.

ISBN 0-7509-2973-1

Typeset in 11/14.5pt Sabon.
Typesetting and origination by
Sutton Publishing Limited.
Printed and bound in England by
J.H. Haynes & Co. Ltd, Sparkford.

# Contents

# Introduction

Monarchies are few and far between in the twenty-first century. Only around a dozen of them remain, together with a few independent principalities and Arab sheikdoms. At one time, monarchy exercised a virtual monopoly of government. Now it appears to be an anachronism, persisting into a democratic world that has largely rejected everything it stands for: privilege and the rights of heredity, class superiority, the prerogatives of wealth, and the concept of monarchs as special, even divine, beings.

There is a fundamental difference between monarchy and its alternative, the republic, which today dominates the governance of the world. As a concept, the republic relies on philosophy and ideology, the use of intellect and reason to change the circumstances of life. Monarchy, on the other hand, appeals to something much deeper in the human psyche: the need to find safety in authority and reassurance in the exercise of that authority by those who can be trusted to preserve an established way of life.

In 1789, the slogan *Liberté, Egalité, Fraternité* said it all for the republic that emerged from the French Revolution. However, in the ancient world which first gave rise to monarchy, this philosophy, predicated on human rights and the dignity of the individual, was not something society could, as yet, afford. Superior strength and intelligence, force of personality and all the other qualities of leadership were much more important in perilous, primitive times when survival was always on the line and the world seemed full of angry gods and spirits bent on human destruction.

In these circumstances, the leaders who emerged were usually those who appeared to have contact with, and some influence over, the unseen forces that governed everyday life. Warriors, priests and others with this special ability became the first monarchs and on the way, their proximity to divine forces gave them a god-like aura. It was a short step from there to the concept of monarchs as divine in themselves.

This is an idea that persists today in traditional societies, such as those of Japan or Nepal, where religions – Shinto and Hinduism respectively – allow for the addition to existing pantheons of new, royal gods. However, this was not possible where monotheism precluded all other deities, as it did among the Jews of ancient Israel or, much later, the Christians of Europe. Israel had its kings, although the Bible makes it clear that God did not approve, on the grounds that He was the only authority they required. Subsequently, the Jews never fully solved the problem of how to incorporate monarchs into a system where their one God was also a 'jealous God'.

Christian Europe, on the other hand, developed a different emphasis to cope with the problem: the Divine Right of Kings, in which monarchs were appointed by, and answerable only to, God. This, though, was not meant to give monarchs a direct line to the deity. There were 'middlemen', as it were – the Pope and the Church in Rome which, in medieval times, claimed the kings of Europe as their vassals and punished them for failures of fealty. Several kings fought hard against these restraints. One of them – Henry II of England – caused the greatest scandal of medieval times when his quarrel with his Archbishop of Canterbury, Thomas Becket, led to Becket's murder in 1170.

Europe's kings did not get a real chance to exert total mastery over their own realms until after the Renaissance began in around 1450. The royal urge for independence was succoured by the revival of ancient Greek and Roman culture, the 'new learning', the development of humanism, which celebrated human abilities and, above all, the serious divisions in the Church which resulted in the breakaway Protestant movement. Ultimately, this produced a more draconian form of monarchy: absolute monarchy in which a king's word was law, his will was unquestioned, his person was hallowed and his decisions were incontrovertible. The monarch who most epitomised this form of monarchy was King Louis XIV of France whose statement 'L'état c'est moi' – 'I am the state' described in a nutshell the basic belief that lay behind absolute rule. It was ironic, though, that the Renaissance also gave rise to those concepts of human rights and the dignity of the individual which ultimately brought down absolute monarchy and did so in a very violent, bloody fashion.

England escaped this fate by settling its account with its monarchs in its own way. Kings and queens in England had never ruled by Divine Right and the Stuart monarchs who attempted it paid a heavy price for their temerity. One, Charles I, was executed in 1649. Another, his son Charles II, spent eleven years in exile before he was able to claim his throne in 1660. His brother, James II, was deposed and driven from his kingdom in 1688.

Although the English experimented with a republic – the short-lived Commonwealth that followed the death of Charles I – they later found an ingenious way of retaining their monarchy while keeping it under parliamentary control. Constitutional monarchy, in which monarchs reigned but did not rule, was first introduced in England in 1689. This, of course, was a full century before the ultimate explosion of protest against absolute monarchy – the French Revolution. The Revolution in its turn gave rise to a mass of liberal uprisings right across Europe in 1848, and these ultimately snowballed so far that absolute monarchy and the Divine Right of Kings ceased to exist in Europe seventy years later.

What followed was the heyday of republican government, which achieved a clean sweep of central and south-east Europe by the mid-twentieth century. However, monarchy and royalty failed to fade into history, as republican lore had foretold. In its constitutional form, monarchy survived to serve as a focus of national loyalty, recasting royalty as social leaders or as celebrities spearheading charities and other good works. In these various ways, monarchy has beaten all the odds and evolved its way into a new millennium where many once presumed it had no place.

# ONE

## *Monarchy in the Ancient World*

Human beings are not equal. If they were, there would never have been any kings, emperors, aristocracies, leaders or anyone else who stood out from the crowd. In our egalitarian times, it may be unfashionable to say so, but nature, which is the driving force in such matters, has never worked on the basis of equality. The lottery of the gene pool from which individuals take their characteristics, abilities and personalities has always ensured that some are better endowed than others. In modern societies, all may be equal before the law. Opportunities are there for everyone. Human rights are, or should be, universal.

However, theory and practice part company before the obvious fact that some are better than others at exploiting the chances offered to them. Leaders have an inborn quality of command which impresses those who lack it. Talent is a mysterious gift, arising from a mixture of intelligence, inheritance and sheer chance. Genius is even more rare.

Nature's inequalities have been of benefit to all societies across the centuries, from the most primitive to our own age of space exploration and advanced technology. In all ages, extraordinary individuals have been required to solve problems, provide hope or inspiration in times of trouble and, when life has been under threat, devise ways of enabling it to continue. In earliest times, rituals, ceremonies, sacrifices and superstitions all had their part to play in mollifying the destructive forces of nature – fire, volcanoes, floods or the strange workings of heavenly bodies. However, it was those who looked as if they could exert control over rampant nature who leapt ahead of the rest and began to forge the brand of personal power that eventually led to the institution of monarchy.

1

Monarchy, especially in Britain, has long been regarded with awe, infused with magic. Royalty is special, almost a race apart, human because royals die like everyone else, but somehow perpetual. This may sound like some fanciful delusion but it is more solidly based in human experience than it sounds.

The ancient medicine man, with his ritual dances, strange gestures and magic potions exerted a strong influence over the members of his tribe, who looked to him to cure their ills or devise a defence against their enemies. Shamans appeared to have the ability to make rain, produce thunder or drive the moon from the face of the sun during total eclipses. Sorcerers could curse and kill from a distance. Today, we would say that the medicine man had some basic medical knowledge not given to all. The shaman knew how to read the sky and realised that the sun in eclipse was only a temporary state. The sorcerer had an inkling of human psychology. But for those unaware of the secrets of such magic, this was impressive – and comforting – stuff.

It was also power, and power where it most mattered. This not only raised these 'magicians' to a special position in society, it raised their families as well. In time, magic became a family business, and a family secret. Oligarchies arose in which magic abilities were thought to pass from one generation to the next.[1] The first heirs to the 'throne' were heirs to tribal magic, with the knowledge and the right to exert power over the tribe. Their abilities ensured their dominance, the dependence of the tribe ensured their continuity.

Shamans may have been working their magic 27,000 years ago or more, when cave painters at Lascaux in France, Altamira in Spain and Panchmarhi in India were making images of the animals they hunted for food. Working in semi-darkness with crude tools and raw pigments, these prehistoric artists achieved a wonderful degree of realism, perspective and skill in the use of colour. These cave paintings were discovered in the late nineteenth century, but only recently was it realised that there was more to them than met the eye.

Many animals were shown pierced with spears. Some paintings were effectively X-ray images, showing the animals' insides. From this and other evidence, the theory grew that prehistoric cave

paintings were a part of a system of sympath[...] [...] to
promote success in the hunt. Situated deep inside the caves, the areas
of the paintings were like temples or shrines where prayers were said
and the appropriate rituals performed.

Quite possibly, the shamans or medicine men presided. The caves,
infused with mystery and an eerie, frightening atmosphere, were the
perfect stage for magic. The small oil lamps that passed for
illumination in prehistoric times flickered among the pools of
darkness. Shadows moved over the walls. The shaman's voice
echoed in and out of the grottoes and uneven surfaces. In this
setting, the paintings could take on a dreamlike air of virtual reality.
Afterwards, the hunters set out, spiritually fortified by the
ceremonies. If the hunt was successful, it was an easy matter to
ascribe its success to the shaman and his rituals – and the images
painted on the cave walls.

Prehistoric cave-dwellings, and their paintings, were not isolated,
however, or if they were, it was not for long. Where the hunting
grounds were fruitful, they attracted numerous families to the area,
and the crowding, inevitably, led to rivalries. Just as inevitably,
rivalries led to war. Most of the early wars arose over food and water
resources or the invasion of territory by neighbouring tribes. The
weapons – stakes, axes, bows and arrows – were already to hand: the
tools that could kill animals could also be turned on enemies. So
could the skills already developed for the hunt: strategy, tactics, or
the nerve to stage ambushes or work the element of surprise.

In these circumstances, the most able, most fearless warriors
would naturally rise to positions of command. They knew by
instinct how and where to attack the enemy, defend a position, work
out a plan of action or inspire trust and confidence in others. How
they knew, where their abilities came from, were part of the mystery
that made them superior.

Wars and winning wars became so vital to the survival of the tribe
that the warrior general soon became the warrior chief. In larger
groupings, he would become the paramount chief or the warrior
king. Somewhere along the way, the proto-kings of prehistoric times
took on the mantle of the shamans and medicine men. Quite

possibly they were descended from them, so that magic and military leadership were powerfully combined in one person.[2]

There was more to this than the rise of one man to the pinnacle of power. The connotations of this rise were of vital importance in the evolution of human society. In *The Golden Bough*, the classic work of comparative religion first published in 1890, Sir James Frazer put it this way:

> The rise of monarchy appears to be an essential condition of the emergence of mankind from savagery. . . . The rise of one man to supreme power enables him to carry through changes in a single lifetime which previously many generations might not have sufficed to effect; and if, as will often happen, he is a man of intellect and energy above the common, he will readily avail himself of the opportunity.
>
> Even the whims and caprices of a tyrant may be of service in breaking the chain of custom which lies so heavy on the savage. And as soon as the tribe . . . yields to the direction of a single strong and resolute mind, it becomes formidable to its neighbours and enters on a career of aggrandisement, which at an early stage of history is often highly favourable to social, industrial, and intellectual progress.[3]

However, the rise of kings was not simply a political development, but one that was intimately bound up with religion and the idea that monarchs enjoyed a line to the gods not given to other mortals. From there, it was easy to see kings as the earthly representatives of the gods, and finally, as gods themselves. These transitions were hardly difficult. The ancient shamans and sorcerers were believed to commune with the gods. This made them into a readymade élite. The gods 'spoke' to them, and only to them, and they conveyed the divine pronouncements to the people.

Kings as warriors had a similar interest in reserving their eminence to themselves and their families. However, the notion that innate talent or genius enabled some to succeed where others failed was rarely in keeping with the thought processes of a superstitious age. Instead, the most obvious explanation was that successful war leaders were personally guided by the gods or spirits. And when the functions of king and priest or magician were combined, there was a dual interest in maintaining the supremacy their skills had enabled them to achieve.

Ultimately, all the most vital elements in life were claimed by, or accorded to, the king. One was the fertility of the soil, which became of cardinal importance once the early hunter-gatherer stage of civilisation gave way to farming. Another was the direction of religious ceremonies, on the principle that if the gods were present in the form of their earthly representatives, the kings, then prayers would be more efficacious. The leadership of armies was a further monopoly and another was the right of kings to choose their own successors. Frequently, although not always, successors were sons of the previous monarch: they became kings in their own right on the premise that heredity had given them the same abilities and qualities as their forebears. In this way, dynasties – the greatest of all monopolies – were established and perpetuated. So was the veneration accorded to monarchs, which was little different from the worship given to the gods. It was therefore in the interests of kings to appear as godlike as possible. In Sumeria, the earliest known civilisation of Mesopotamia, monarchs buttressed their power by laying claim to divinity. This, they said, came to them at birth from the gods and goddesses who were their parents. They also took on the mantle of established deities and were worshipped, in addition, as incarnations of Tammuz, the god of fertility, or as the earthly lieutenants of Ishtar, the goddess of heaven. Later, in the twenty-third century BC, Sargon, King of Akkad, asserted his divinity towards the end of his reign, after his military conquests had created the first great empire in Mesopotamia.

In the ancient world, the godly status of kings was nowhere more elaborately displayed than in Egypt. The divine pharaoh was an integral part of the Egyptian religion and was thought to be the reincarnation of Horus, son of the god Osiris. It was from Osiris that the pharaohs inherited their ability to live after death. With the pharaoh as its centrepiece, the civilisation of Ancient Egypt institutionalised the powers of the ancient shamans and sorcerers.

According to Dr Henri Frankfort, the Dutch-born Egyptologist: 'Kingship in Egypt remained the channel through which the powers of Nature flow into the body politic, to bring human endeavour to fruition.'

This exalted function was maintained even after the concept of kingship changed during the Middle Kingdom (2080–1640 BC): the pharaohs, it was now believed, were not in themselves divine but were appointed by and answerable to the gods. This was the origin of the Divine Right of Kings, which later saw its greatest days, and greatest disasters, in Europe.

Whether as gods or divine appointees, the pharaohs possessed qualities not given to ordinary mortals, such as *Ka* or vital energy. They were expected to dispense *maat* – justice, stability and truth – maintain the cycle of the seasons and perpetuate the divine order. They were the source of the continuing relationship between nature and human beings, which was first established by Osiris. Through their power, they regulated the passage of the sun through the sky from sunrise to sunset. Through them, the River Nile ebbed and flowed.

The importance of the divine pharaohs could hardly have been greater. If anything, they regarded themselves as even mightier than the gods. In the twentieth century BC, Pharaoh Amenemhet I, whose divine name, Wehem-masul, meant 'he who repeats births', set out the all-embracing extent of his powers when he said: 'I was the one who produced barley. The Nile respected me at every defile. None hungered in my years or thirsted in them. Men dwelt in peace through that which I wrought.'

Amenemhet, originally a vizier of humble origins and a usurper, was still subject to the cut and thrust of politics and the rivalries inherent in the use of power: a 'harem conspiracy' was brewed against him and he was assassinated by his bodyguards in 1962 BC. However, in ancient Egypt, death was not the end. A dead pharaoh, it was believed, was still capable of caring for his people and exercising his powers for their benefit in the afterlife. Divinity was also his legacy: Amenemhet's son, Senusret I, automatically assumed his father's godly status when he succeeded him.

The perception of the pharaoh as god depended, of course, on the continual existence and worship of the ancient Egyptian pantheon. This was why the priests in the fourteenth century BC reacted so violently when the maverick pharaoh Amenhotep IV, better known as Akhenaten, the 'pious son of Aten', sought to alter the basis of ancient Egyptian religion. In place of a pantheon of gods, Akhenaten chose to worship only one, the sun god Aten, later known as Aten-Ra. Akhenaten retained his divinity as pharaoh and presented himself as the mediator between Aten and the Egyptian people.

The dislocation of Egyptian spiritual life was immense. Amun, the supreme creator god, was demoted. The cult of Osiris was banned. The names of all other Egyptian deities were erased from the walls of temples. All previous religious festivals were cancelled. The main temple at Tell-el-Amarna was realigned with a valley through which the sun first appeared at daybreak: unlike the temples of Amun, they were left open to the sky – and the sun.

However, even the divine pharaoh could not shift the huge weight of traditional worship and devotion given to the established gods. Ordinary Egyptians refused to alter their beliefs. The priests pronounced Akhenaten's changes blasphemous and Akhenaten himself, a heretic. After his death in around 1336 BC, he was buried in a small, undecorated tomb. The priests of Amun, who returned to power in the reign of his successor, Tutankhamen, defaced the name and image of Akhenaten wherever they occurred, and destroyed the monuments he had built. The Egyptians were never again diverted from their ancient beliefs until the advent of Christianity in the first century AD. Up to that time the divine status and all-embracing powers of the pharaohs continued to derive from the traditional gods.

Much later, royal, or rather imperial, divinity made its appearance in ancient Rome. Shortly after 29 BC, Gaius Julius Caesar Octavianus, great-nephew and adopted son of Julius Caesar, achieved power: although he never claimed the title, contenting himself with *pater patriae*, father of the people, or *princeps*, first citizen, Octavianus eventually assumed the status of Rome's first emperor under the new name of Augustus. After their deaths, Augustus and several of his successors were proclaimed gods. Special temples were erected

7

dedicated to their worship. The Romans were generally tolerant about religion, and faiths that had originated all over the Empire were permissible in Rome. Each faith was allowed its own temple. However, there was one proviso: all of them had to acknowledge the Roman emperors as gods. Only the Jews, with their devotion to Yahweh, the one and only God, refused to obey. The tone was set by Julius Caesar, who was made a god after the conspirators who murdered him in 44 BC were caught and punished. The divinity of the Roman emperors lasted for three centuries: they were still being worshipped in western Asia and Egypt when the Roman Empire turned Christian after 313 AD.

The king as god was not a principle confined to a single part of the world. It was global. It arose in places far away from the civilisations of Mesopotamia, China, India or Rome and did so without any known contact. In Aztec Mexico, for example, the Great Speaker, or *tlatoani*, was regarded as divine, and elaborate precautions were taken to avoid looking them in the face. This belief was similar to that of the ancient Jews that to look on the face of God was to invite death. In addition, the *tlatoani* was considered so sacred that his feet were not supposed to touch the ground. This accounted for the behaviour of the *tetecuhtin*, the Aztec nobles, who carried the litter of the Great Speaker Moctezuma Xoyoctzin, better known as Montezuma, at his first meeting with Hernan Cortés, the Spanish conquistador who invaded Mexico in November 1519:

'Montezuma descended from his litter,' wrote Bernal Diaz del Castillo, one of Cortés' conquistadores, 'and . . . great [lords] supported him beneath a marvellously rich canopy of green feathers, decorated with gold work, silver [and] pearls. It was a marvellous sight. The great Montezuma was magnificently clad . . . and wore sandals . . . the soles of which were of gold and the upper parts ornamented with precious stones. . . . Many more lords . . . walked before [him] sweeping the ground on which he was to tread and laying down cloaks so that his feet should not touch the earth. Not one of these [lords] dared to look him in the face.'

Elsewhere in pre-Hispanic America, in Tahuantinsuyu – the 'Land of the Four Quarters' better known as Inca Peru – the Sapa Inca or

Supreme Lord was thought to be so exalted that no one was fit to eat meals with him. Instead, he ate alone, twice a day at eight in the morning and at nightfall, taking his food with his fingers from gold and silver dishes held for him by handmaidens. If any gravy or pieces of food fell on the Sapa Inca's fine vicuna wool tunic, he immediately changed into another garment. The soiled tunic was burned. If there were any of his hairs on his clothing, his servants would eat them so that no one could ever touch any part of his sacred body.

As with the Aztec *tlatoani*, it was forbidden to look directly at the Sapa Inca. Often, when he received visitors, attendants would hold a purple cloth veil in front of him so that no one could gaze upon his face. Customs like these inculcated awe and dread in all who came into the royal presence. In 1532, when another Spanish conquistador, Francisco Pizarro, brought a small group of men to the Inca capital Cuzco, one of them, a fifteen-year-old page called Pedro Pizarro saw what happened when a provincial governor arrived late at the palace of the Sapa Inca Atahualpa.

'The [Sapa] Inca gave [the governor] the Lord of the Huaylas, limited time in which to go to his estates and return.' Pedro Pizarro wrote forty years later in his *Discovery and Conquest of the Kingdoms of Peru*. 'He took rather longer, and when he came back, he brought a gift of fruit and arrived in the Inca's presence. The Lord of the Huaylas began to tremble in such a manner before the Inca that he was unable to remain on his feet.'

This reaction was hardly surprising when the Sapa Inca was regarded as the son of the sun god, Inti. Shining brilliantly in the sky, Inti represented Viracocha, the giver of all life and owner of everything and everyone on Earth. It followed that everything under the sun belonged to the Sapa Inca. The land was his, the soil was his, the people were his property, the vast wealth of gold, which was called 'the sweat of the Sun' belonged to him, and so did the silver, 'the tears of the Moon'.

Inevitably, there were risks involved in loading so much power and obligation on to monarchs that they became responsible for the ongoing survival of their subjects.[4] In some parts of the world, this led to a savage conclusion. Once a king aged and his health declined, the well-being of the whole community was in danger. The fertility of the soil, for which the king was responsible, declined with him. The solution was to kill the ageing king and put a younger, more vigorous successor in his place.

In this context, the soul was bound up with the body. A feeble body meant a feeble soul. It was thought much better to kill a king before his soul weakened too far, to catch it as it emerged at the moment of death and transfer it to his young successor. This killing of the god-king occurred all over the ancient world. It was widely believed that if a monarch were allowed to die a natural death, disaster was imminent, although the deed itself was normally left until almost the last moment.

In ancient Cambodia, for example, when the elders decided that a sick monarch was not going to recover, he was stabbed to death. In the Congo of central Africa, where the chief, the *Chitomé*, was regarded as sole sustainer of the earth and its benefits, his natural death meant the end of the world. To avert this catastrophe, a dying chief was killed by his chosen successor.

This, it appears, was not simply done with the victim's assent: the *Chitomé* himself ordered that he die in this fashion. In 1732, Father Merolla de la Sorrento, an Italian missionary in Africa, explained the ramifications of the custom in his *Relazione del Viaggio nel regno di Congo* (Account of a Journey in the Kingdom of Congo).

Let us pass to the death of the magicians, who often die a violent death and that for the most part voluntarily. I shall speak only of the . . . *Ganga Chitomé*, being the reputed god of the earth. The first fruits of all the crops are offered to him as his due, because they are thought to be produced by his power. . . . He asserts that his body cannot die a natural death, and therefore when he knows he is near the end of his days, whether it is brought about by sickness or age . . . he calls on one of his disciples to whom he wishes to communicate his power, in order that he may succeed him. And having made him tie a noose to his neck, he commands him to strangle him, or to knock him on the head with a great cudgel and kill him. His disciple obeys. . . . This tragedy is enacted in public, in order that his successor may be manifested, who hath the power of fertilising the earth, the power having been imparted to him by the deceased; otherwise, so they say, the earth would remain barren and the world would perish.[5]

In Aztec Mexico, the killing of kings was observed in a ritualised form. The victim was not the *tlatoani* but a substitute king who was chosen for disposal at the annual Festival of Tezcatlipoca, one of the Aztec creator-gods. A young man of sixteen or seventeen was selected to be 'King for a Year'.

During that year, in Tenochtitlan, the Aztec capital situated on Lake Texcoco, he was pampered in every way possible. He was taught how to play the flute and was given splendid garments to wear. He had gold bangles to decorate his arms and gold bells to wear around his legs. He was garlanded with flowers and had eight attendants to wait on him and grant his every wish. His wishes included as many young women as bedmates as he could manage during his year as 'king'.

Some three weeks before the next Festival of Tezcatlipoca, the young man was dressed as a warrior chieftain. A week of feasting and dancing preceded the festival itself. The 'king' was the centrepiece of the celebrations. Then, on the day of the festival, the 'king' stepped into a canoe and was paddled to a small temple on the shore of Lake Texcoco. As he walked towards the temple steps, he broke all the flutes he had played during his year of leisure and pleasure. He mounted the steps and became the latest of the thousands of human sacrifices offered by the *tlenamacac*, the élite priests whose daily task it was to rip open chests and offer the still-beating hearts to the sun god Huitzilopochtli.[6] Immediately, another young man was chosen to take the dead 'king's' place and to die in the same way at the next year's festival.

King-killing was most common in Africa where, in pre-colonial times, there were hundreds of small kingdoms, all of them relying for survival on the moods of the gods and many of them prepared, it seems, to sacrifice their monarchs to ensure divine blessing. In this context, a gruesome fate awaited kings of Fazoql, in the valley of the

Blue Nile. One of their duties was to dispense justice, sitting beneath a tree designated for the purpose. However, if a king failed to appear 'in court' for three days in succession, through illness or some other reason, his relatives and ministers declared him *persona non grata*. He was no longer of use to his people, his country and even to his animals. It followed that he had to be hanged. This, though, was not a simple execution. The noose was equipped with two sharp razors so that as the rope closed tight around the king's neck, his throat was cut. The killing of the kings of Fazoql was still going on in the nineteenth century.

The principle of king-killing could, of course, be abused. In Meroe, an ancient Ethiopian kingdom dating from around 300 BC, the priests decided whether the king should live or die. The ostensible reason was that an oracle from the gods had decreed the king's death. More practical purposes could have been personal, political or dynastic. Priests with another, possibly more pliant, king in mind could use this custom to get rid of a monarch who was less agreeable to them. However that may be, when the order went out, kings were expected to obey, and for many centuries they did so. Then, some time in the mid-third century BC, according to the Greek historian Diodorus Siculus, a king came to the throne of Meroe with no intention of committing royal suicide on the say-so of his priests. He was Arkamani, whose eventual grave was the first of the pyramid tombs of Meroe. Arkamani, also known as Ergamenes, had been educated in Greece and had imbibed Greek ideas of individualism, free will and logical thinking. A king like this was unlikely to be a slave of custom, nor was he. When Arkamani received the order to kill himself, he went down to the temple, accompanied by a troop of armed soldiers. This time, it was the priests, not the king, who died.

Elsewhere in the ancient world, the kings as gods, their responsibilities and their duty to die for the sake of the community were not universal. For instance, the claims to divinity of the early kings in Sumeria did not spread widely among the later kingdoms of Mesopotamia. In a different, more practical tradition, councils of elders chose kings only in times of emergency, much as the Romans later chose their dictators. The royal role was to solve crises and

12

preserve the people. The royal mission was seen as divine, but not the kings themselves. This concept of kingship left evidence in the bas reliefs and statues that celebrated Mesopotamia's monarchs: unlike the Egyptian pharaoh-gods, they were carved life-size rather than oversize.

Divine kingship – in fact kingship itself – did not have much currency in ancient Greece, either. This land of sturdily republican city states which fostered the first stirrings of democracy was unlikely to want much to do with god-kings. In the fourth century BC, even Alexander III of Macedon – Alexander the Great – got short shrift when he attempted to assert his divinity with the liberty-loving Greeks. Chauvinism played its part. The Greeks had a great sense of superiority *vis à vis* the Macedonians, whom they regarded as barbarians. The Athenian politician and orator Demosthenes went so far as to call King Philip II, Alexander's father, a 'pestilent knave from . . . a district [where] we have not yet been able to purchase a decent slave.'

The autocratic Alexander was not typical of Macedonian royalty. Macedonian kings were not supreme lords, divine or otherwise. They were elected monarchs, whose appointment was confirmed by the acclamation of the military. They could be voted out of office if they lost popular loyalty and their powers were constitutional, not absolute. Under this system, kings were *primus inter pares*, first among equals, and they had to prove themselves worthy of their royal authority on a regular basis. There was no pomp, no pageantry and no royal regalia until it was introduced by Alexander. Kings of Macedonia did not even have a superior form of dress: they wore the same clothes as the *hetairoi*, the nobility.

Alexander's view of his position in life was far too exalted to be confined by such ideas. He believed that divine blood coursed through his veins and he claimed descent from the legendary Greek heroes Achilles and Herakles. He even referred to his father Philip II as 'my so-called father'. It followed that Alexander was much more despotic and demanded much more veneration than the Macedonian concept of kingship ever envisaged, or the Greeks were willing to give.

Monarchy in Greece had barely outlasted the eighth century BC, 400 years before Alexander was born. Once considered suited only to the large tribal group, kingship gave way to rule by councils of elders. Starting on the island of Crete, this type of government spread to mainland Greece, where it was first taken up in Sparta. Where monarchy survived, as in Laconia, the kings were military and religious heads, but the elders held powers that were equal to theirs. Long before Alexander, therefore, the Greeks had become accustomed to what might be called 'rule by committee', a committee whose members were either elected or chosen by acclamation.

The picture changed, however, when Philip of Macedon won supremacy over the Greek city states after a long struggle lasting almost twenty years. By 338 BC, Philip had prevailed but two years later, he was assassinated. Alexander, then only twenty years old, succeeded his father as king, but the Greek city states refused to accept him. With the connivance of Athens and other states, the state of Thebes rose in revolt in 336 BC and again the following year. Alexander's answer was to destroy Thebes, sell its people into slavery and parcel out the Theban lands among its neighbours.

After this, the Greeks had no option but to submit to Alexander's military genius. At the Diet of Corinth, all the states, except for Sparta, elected him as *Hēgemōn Autokrator*, sole leader, for a campaign designed to free the Greek colonies in Ionia from Persian rule. Subsequently, the city states – some out of gratitude, but others unwillingly – granted Alexander the 'godlike honours' he demanded of them. Doubtless to their relief, Alexander's imperial ambitions soon took him far away from Greece as he embarked on the conquest of a vast empire that stretched to the edge of the then known world, along the coast of India. Alexander died in 323 BC, aged thirty-two. The emissaries the Greeks sent to his bedside wore crowns, possibly in his honour, but maybe as a derisory comment on his royal ambitions.

The Greek reason for resisting the idea of the god-king had been political and philosophical. A much stronger challenge, based on religious principles, arose in ancient Israel. This was due to the nature of Yahweh, who demanded from the Jews a much stricter brand of obedience than any other deity imposed on worshippers. At the very start of the Jews' relationship with Yahweh, He demanded exclusive rights to worship: this fundamental rule was set out in the Book of Exodus which recounts how Yahweh masterminded the escape of the Jews from slavery in Egypt: 'I am the Lord thy God, which have brought thee out of the land of Egypt, out of the house of bondage. Thou shalt have no other gods before me. Thou shalt not make unto thee any graven image, or any likeness of any thing that is in heaven above, or that is in the earth beneath, or that is in the water under the earth.'[7]

However, obedience to Yahweh's requirements was never easy and rarely complete. The Bible is full of accounts showing how the Jews constantly strayed from the straight and narrow, how they sought to emulate their neighbours against the wishes of Yahweh, how they worshipped pagan gods and how the prophets delivered regular warnings about the dire penalties all this would incur.

Some of the strongest warnings concerned the Jews' demand for a king. The Jews had no tradition of ancient shamans, medicine men or magicians and consequently their priests never evolved into kings or founded royal dynasties. In the early days in ancient Israel, the loose-knit tribes were ruled by 'judges' who were chiefly military leaders and scored some success in fending off attacks by neighbouring tribes. From time to time 'deliverers' also arose to get the Jews out of trouble. In ancient times, small, weak states had a poor future in Mesopotamia and the adjacent lands. Sooner or later, they were overrun and absorbed by neighbours with more muscle and better armies. To avert this fate, the Jews decided they must have a king to centralise government, build up the nation's defences and confront their enemies on more equal terms.

This was not an idea that found much favour with Yahweh or the Prophet Samuel. Israel was a theocracy. Monarchy was an intruder, introducing a rival, secular system of government. By their very nature, the two were mutually exclusive. Samuel saw immediately the paradox of monarchy in a land where Yahweh ruled supreme and His laws were paramount. He predicted that Israel would bitterly regret the day it acquired a king. Taking examples from the despotic regimes of surrounding states, he warned the Israelites of what a king would do. It was not an agreeable forecast:

> This will be the manner of the king that shall reign over you. He will take your sons, and appoint them for himself, for his chariots, and to be his horsemen; and some shall run before his chariots. . . . And he will take your fields, and your vineyards, and your oliveyards, even the best of them, and give them to his servants. . . . He will take the tenth of your sheep: and ye shall be his servants. And ye shall cry out in that day because of your king which ye shall have chosen. . . .

Samuel's warning was ignored. The Jews insisted on a king and they got one in the shape of Saul, a Benjamite who came from one of the smallest of the twelve tribes of Israel. 'Saul' meant 'requested' but, if the Israelites thought they were going to have a king like other kings, they were mistaken.

King Saul was a poor imitation of the grandeur and eminence of other monarchs. He had no palace. He conducted government business from beneath a tree in Gibeah, his home city. He created no body of officials, advisers or civil servants. He had no appreciable standing army and those soldiers he did command were poorly equipped. He was not even full-time, but combined kingship with his work as a farmer.

Unlike other monarchs in the ancient world, Saul was not able to claim divinity or even its offshoot, the Divine Right of Kings. Instead, Saul had to prove himself. Fortunately, a military emergency allowed him to gain the prestige he required. When Jabesh-gilead, a town close to the River Jordan, was besieged by the Ammonites, the inhabitants offered to surrender, only to find to their horror that if they did so, then the Ammonite leader Nahash intended to put out their right eyes. Saul gathered his army and drove the Ammonites away. The people of Jabesh-gilead – and their right eyes – were saved.

Afterwards, Saul was equally successful in his wars against intrusive neighbours such as the Moabites. However, the practical, secular concerns of monarchy soon began to clash with Saul's religious obligations. In the Bible, he is shown as constantly failing to follow divine instructions as imparted to him by the prophet Samuel. Saul's final act of disobedience illustrates the difficulties inherent in being a king and a military commander while remaining under the tutelage of God.

Confronted by an immense Philistine army of 30,000 chariots and 6,000 horsemen at Gilgal, Saul was so fearful of being annihilated that he broke the rules. Samuel had told Saul to wait a week, until he arrived to make the necessary burnt offerings before the battle. Samuel came late and Saul, fearful of waiting any longer, made the burnt offerings to God himself. Saul's punishment for his disobedience was the loss of his kingdom.

God had already chosen another king to replace Saul – David, the youngest son of Jesse of the tribe of Judah. David was, as yet, too young to rule. Saul therefore retained his throne, but there was no more guidance from God. Saul became obsessively jealous of David and suffered paralysing bouts of melancholy. He tried, but failed, to kill David on several occasions. David, however, did not have to wait long for his throne. In 1048 BC, two years after he became king, Saul faced the Philistines again in a last, fatal battle at Gilboa. By this time, Samuel was dead. With no way of communicating with God, Who refused to answer his prayers, Saul resorted to a medium, the witch of Endor. At the king's request, she raised the spirit of Samuel. Samuel was not best pleased to be disturbed and told Saul that he had brought this latest crisis on himself: 'Wherefore then dost thou ask of me, seeing the Lord is departed from thee, and is become thine enemy? . . . Because thou obeyest not the voice of the Lord, therefore hath the Lord done this thing unto thee this day. Moreover the Lord will also deliver Israel with thee into the hand of the Philistines: and tomorrow shalt thou and thy sons be with me'.[8]

Shortly afterwards, at the Battle of Gilboa, Saul's army was decimated by the Philistines and the king and his son Jonathan were killed. Their corpses were beheaded and their bodies hung from the walls of the Philistine town of Beth-shan.

17

David was much more of a king in the splendid, heroic mould the Jews probably had in mind when they first demanded a monarch. David captured Jerusalem from the Canaanites. He built it up into a magnificent city, with a palace for himself and a splendid temple. He finally vanquished the Philistines, who never again posed a threat to Israel. One conquest followed another – Edom, Moab, Ammon, Aram, Damascus, the Valley of Jezreel – until David had transformed what had been a weak, minor state into a vast empire. David himself became a hero-king of the highest order, a reputation he still retains among Jews today.

On the way, however, David's conduct of the wars spilled over into brutality. The fate of the Moabites, for example, was, by any standards, an atrocity.

> And he smote Moab, and measured them with a line, casting them down to the ground; even with two lines measured he put to death, and with one full line, to keep alive. . . . David smote also Hadadezer, the son of Rehob, king of Zobah, as he went to recover his border at the river Euphrates. And David took from him a thousand chariots, and seven hundred horsemen, and twenty thousand footmen: and David [killed] all the chariot horses, but reserved [some] of them for an hundred chariots. And when the Syrians of Damascus came to succour Hadadezer king of Zobah, David slew of the Syrians two and twenty thousand men.[9]

Despite the violence and bloodletting that accompanied David's imperial wars, the Biblical account makes it clear that he retained the favour of God and received His protection wherever he went. However, some events in David's personal life were less acceptable. David committed adultery with Bathsheba, having first engineered the death of her husband, Uriah the Hittite. Despite taking an oath not to harm the family of the late King Saul, David had seven of Saul's descendants killed. The sins of the father appeared to devolve on his children. For example, David's eldest son Amnon seduced his half-sister Tamar. The family history also included fratricide, rebellion and treachery.

David's son and successor Solomon, who came to the throne in around 965 BC, built up a tremendous reputation for his wisdom, his wealth, his ambitious – and expensive – building projects and the glory he brought to the name of Israel. Like his father, Solomon was an absolute ruler and as his reign proceeded, he began to resemble an eastern potentate rather than a king bound to the laws of God.

Behind Solomon's lustrous image lay a vengeful despot who began his reign by eliminating his rivals. Solomon suspected his half brother Adonijah of planning to lay claim to the throne. The plot, if it existed at all, cost Adonijah his life. Joab, formerly David's commander-in-chief of the army, fell foul of Solomon and was murdered by the king's agents while in sanctuary at the temple. Solomon's extensive harem of some 700 wives and 300 concubines contravened the divine instruction that Jewish males should not marry or have relations with non-Jews.[10] Solomon not only married outside his faith several times, but provided his non-Jewish brides with their own chapels where they could worship their pagan gods. Of all the sins committed by the people of Israel as recorded in the Bible, worshipping, or permitting the worship, of idols was the greatest of them all.

The glory of King Solomon came at a very high price, and it was the people of Israel who paid it. The royal taxes were very heavy. These taxes were not necessarily in monetary form. On one occasion, twenty cities and their populations were turned over to King Hiram of Tyre, who provided large quantities of wood – the famous cedars of Lebanon – for Solomon's mammoth building projects. The building work was so extensive that the underclass of Canaanites living in Israel was too small to provide all the labour required. Solomon therefore used the *corvée*, forced labour, which imposed servitude on 30,000 of his Jewish subjects. They spent one month in three working for King Hiram of Tyre.

When Solomon died in around 926 BC, ten of the twelve tribes of Israel seized their chance of escaping the royal yoke. Rather than accept Solomon's son, Rehoboam, as their next monarch, the ten tribes seceded and set up a kingdom, and a king, of their own. The division of a once united realm into the Kingdom of Israel in the north and the Kingdom of Judah in the south was the end of King David's vast empire. All its territory was lost by the early ninth century BC and the Jews in both kingdoms were back where they started, as small states vulnerable to the depredations of their neighbours. Most damaging of all, the Jews lost military capability and from that point onwards, eventual disaster was certain.

In 722 BC, the Assyrians, then at the apex of their power as the world's first military state, overran Israel and scattered its population throughout their empire. Fresh conquest by the Babylonians and their capture of Jerusalem in 586 BC resulted in an exile that lasted nearly fifty years. The Jews returned home in 539 BC, but subsequently, they were conquered again, this time by Alexander the Great.

Later, the Jews regained their independence – and their kings – when the Maccabean dynasty freed Israel from foreign domination in 142 BC. However, the interval lasted only eighty years before the Romans arrived. In AD 70, after years of rebellion, which they suppressed with their customary ruthlessness, the Romans changed the name of the country to Palestine and ordered the Jews to leave. Almost two thousand years passed before they returned.

This, no doubt, was what Samuel had meant when he said that the Jews would rue the day they asked for a king.

# TWO

## *Monarchy in Asia*

Nowhere in the world has the concept of divine monarchy lasted longer than in Asia. An instance of its power was revealed in 1945 after the defeat of Japan in the Second World War, when the victorious Americans and their allies demanded that Emperor Hirohito renounce his status as a god. Japan was in ruins, its economy destroyed, its armed forces decimated and two of its cities, Hiroshima and Nagasaki, blasted, burned and poisoned by atomic bombs. Hirohito, whose divinity derived from his direct descent from the Shinto sun goddess Amaterasu Omikami, had no option but to concur.

Nevertheless, many of his subjects, especially the older ones, refused to accept his mortality. Some could not reconcile themselves to the shocking reality of a god turned mortal; they committed *seppuku*, ritual suicide, rather than live with it. According to Harold Nicolson, writing in 1962, the mere presence of such a godly being in Tokyo could reduce ordinary Japanese to fear and trembling. Just passing by the moat that fronts the imperial palace produced an attitude of awe and reverence.[1]

Likewise, in Nepal, the late King Birendra, murdered in 2001 with several members of his family by his son, Crown Prince Deependra, was widely regarded as the reincarnation of the Hindu god Vishnu. The advent of a constitutional monarchy, forced on Birendra in 1990 by democratic elements in Nepal, took nothing away from this age-old belief.

In Thailand, too, King Bhumibhol Ayulaydej is regarded as semi-divine, a creature apart, despite the fact that since his accession to the throne in 1946, intervals of democracy interspersed with military coups have reduced him politically to the status of a figurehead.

'He is considered to be so high, so much above the ordinary run of people, a moral leader, that one simply does not talk about being related to him', said Narisa Chakrabongse, a second cousin of the king. Narisa, who was educated in the royal palace at Bangkok with the king's children, was speaking in 1995.

Unlike the Japanese and also the Chinese monarchies, which go back beyond prehistory into legend, the Thai monarchy is of relatively recent origin, dating from 1238, when the Sukhothai kingdom declared itself independent. Today, the Sukhothai era is regarded as the 'good old days', when Thailand was a place of peace and plenty, with a contented population governed by just, paternalistic kings. The facts were rather more brutal than that. The Sukhothai realm had to fight hard to retain its freedom, first against the Khmer Empire of Cambodia, next against the invading Burmese and after that against encroachments by Europeans.

First in were the Portuguese who gained a head start over other Europeans by discovering the sea route to Asia round the coast of Africa in 1497–8. The first Portuguese traders reached Siam – as Thailand was then known – as early as 1511. Traders of other nationalities – the Dutch, the English and the Spaniards, as well as the Chinese and the Japanese – soon arrived in South-East Asia to exploit the rumoured riches of the area and within a century and a half the Siamese kings had assumed a monopoly of foreign trade. Unfortunately, royal control did not extend to the activities of missionaries, nor did it have much effect on the ambitions of military advisers who were invited in to impart to the Siamese their knowledge of modern warfare. Before long, however, advice and aid began to look too much like a religious takeover bid on the one hand, and colonisation on the other. As a result, after 1690, the foreigners were expelled and Siam went into self-imposed isolation from the outside world for more than a century.

The established Siamese royalty did not survive the years of isolation. Total disaster overwhelmed them after 1767, when the Burmese invaded Siam, besieged and later burned the capital, Ayutthaya, and slaughtered members of the ruling family. Those royals who remained alive were taken back to Burma, along with large quantities of booty and 90,000 other captives. Siam was left in a state of anarchy and civil war, which lasted fifteen years until General Phraya Chakri took control in 1782 and raised himself to royal status by declaring the start of his reign as King Rama I.

By this time, European presence in Asia had passed the transient stage, when individual traders or missionaries established themselves in outposts far from home. The Europeans – especially the British and the French – were moving into Asia in earnest. During the nineteenth century, Siam found itself hemmed in on two fronts: in 1852, Burma, to the west, became a British protectorate, followed by the establishment of French rule to the east, in Cambodia in 1863 and Laos thirty years later.

King Mongkut, Rama IV, king of Siam from 1851 to 1868, had already seen this situation coming and he had before him a fearful example of what could happen when Europeans encountered opposition to their will. In 1842, the emperor of China had refused to give Europeans trading rights and the result was a war, the first Opium War, in which the antiquated Chinese forces were utterly crushed. After that, the Europeans had forced the emperor to give them so many rights and privileges that they were able to do virtually as they pleased in China. The second Opium War of 1856–60 forced even more concessions from the emperor until China was wide open for European exploitation and its rulers helpless to prevent it.

Mongkut had no intention of letting the Chakri dynasty fall into the same trap. The Chinese emperor had clung to the ancient traditions for far too long, including the historical Chinese disdain for foreigners and all their works. Unlike him, Mongkut realised the importance of modernising and employed European advisers to help him modernise the Siamese government, lawcourts and military. It was a tremendous task. Siam was intensely backward, with no system of communications, a peasant economy and only ox carts and elephants for transport. When Mongkut's son, King Chulalongkorn, Rama V, succeeded to the throne in 1868, he realised, like his father, that the acquisitive, ruthless Western world could not be ignored. Unusually for Asian monarchs of the time,

Chulalongkorn embarked on a series of travels to the major western countries. He studied and absorbed western culture, traditions, political organisation and technology and returned to Siam convinced, like his father, that only by continuing to modernise his kingdom could he hope to save it from colonisation. At the same time, Chulalongkorn fully realised how careful he had to be. Colonisation was much more than foreign armies marching in and taking over by force: there were more subtle methods, which could be undetectable until it was too late. For example, when the English queen, Victoria, proposed that the British East India Company construct a railway in Siam, this immediately put Chulalongkorn on his guard. Technological aid, especially for something so important to a country's development as a railway network, was a back-door way to colonisation. The king therefore politely turned the offer down, saying: 'Siam is not yet ready for a railway due to insufficient economy and a relatively low population. The ox cart is the most common form of transport, and [it is] quite sufficient for now.'

Behind this pretence that the time was not yet right, Chulalongkorn made approaches to other European nations and asked them to put in bids and plans for a railway system. Eventually, the king was able to pick and choose between them, giving the task to a combination of several countries. None of them was allowed enough leverage to make an attempt on Siamese sovereignty. King Chulalongkorn also devised his own personal method of ensuring stable, continuous government; he provided his own ministers, officials and civil service by fathering an enormous family. His many wives and concubines produced seventy-seven children – thirty-three sons and forty-four daughters. This way, Chulalongkorn could place blood relatives and in-laws in important posts throughout Siam and, through his children's marriages, secure political support from the country's foremost families.

Eventually, Chulalongkorn transformed his kingdom from a backward country weighed down by antiquated traditions into a state that was modernised by choice rather than by force. Ironically, though, Chulalongkorn's reforms did not include the westernisation of the monarchy itself. The constitutional monarchy of present-day

Thailand did not transpire until 1932. Its democratic constitution dates from only 1974 and even then, there was an echo of the old absolutist ways in the law that forbade any criticism of the 'divine' king or the monarchy.

All the same, among the Asian monarchies, divinity was not seen as *carte blanche* to exercise the royal will without restraint. The Maurya, Gupta and Rajput monarchs of India were regarded as divine in origin and the Rajputs traced their ancestry back to the sun, moon and fire gods. In all these monarchies, the king was a manifestation of the gods on Earth. This, however, laid on him very specific responsibilities which were spelled out in great detail as early as 250 BC in the Hindu text, the *Arthashastra*.

> By overthrowing the aggregate of the six enemies – lust, anger, greed, vanity, haughtiness, and overjoy – he shall restrain the organs of sense; acquire wisdom by keeping company with the aged . . . establish safety and security by being ever active; maintain his subjects in the observance of their respective duties by exercising authority; keep up his personal discipline by receiving lessons in the sciences; and endear himself to the people by bringing them in contact with wealth and doing good to them. . . . If a king is energetic, his subjects will be equally energetic. If he is reckless, they will not only be reckless likewise, but also eat into his works. Besides, a reckless king will easily fall into the hands of his enemies. Hence the king shall ever be wakeful.[2]

The *Arthashastra*, however, did not confine itself to generalisations. Very specific rules were laid down for the apportioning of the royal day.

> He shall divide both the day and the night into eight *nalikas* [1.5 hours]. . . . Of these divisions, during the first one-eighth part of the day, he shall post watchmen and attend to the accounts of receipts and expenditure; during the second part, he shall look to the affairs of both citizens and country people; during the third, he shall not only receive revenue in gold, but also attend to the

appointments of superintendents; . . . during the fifth, he shall correspond in writs with the assembly of his ministers, and receive the secret information gathered by his spies; during the sixth, he may engage himself in his favourite amusements or in self-deliberation; during the seventh, he shall superintend elephants, horses, chariots and infantry; and during the eighth part, he shall consider various plans of military operations with his commander-in-chief. At the close of the day he shall observe the evening prayer. . . .[3]

Although the Muslim Mughals (who first invaded and conquered northern India after 1526) were monotheists, they found it politic to adopt the same divinity as their Hindu predecessors. Zahi ud-din Muhamed, better known as the Emperor Babur was, in fact, a descendant of the famed Mongol leaders Genghis Khan and Tamerlane but recognised the divine or semi-divine ruler as a figure his new subjects would find it most easy to accept. The Mughal emperors were therefore regarded as the shadow of Allah on Earth, or alternatively as the 'emanation of God's light'. They did not rest on their divine laurels, however. Islam had no qualms about lavish displays of wealth and the rich were just as acceptable to Allah as the poor. These ideas set the Mughals free to display their wealth in every conceivable way. Their palaces were made of delicately carved marble encrusted with jewels and decorated with elegant motifs. The imperial courts were staffed by superbly dressed, heavily bejewelled officials and the emperor himself was the epitome of splendour. Dressed in rich brocades and silks, his turbans featured ropes of pearls. Row upon row of jewelled necklaces hung around his neck.

Shah Jehan, the Mughal emperor who built the famous Taj Mahal between 1630 and 1653, used to conduct state business from the Peacock Throne, so called because of the two jewelled peacocks that stood below the umbrella. It was said that the famous Koh-i-Noor diamond, which was part of the booty won by Babur in 1526, went to form one of the peacock's eyes. All this ostentation was quite deliberate. The more dazzling an emperor's appearance and surroundings, the more officials and servants attended upon him, the more his power and authority were underlined. Stupendous wealth was also on show every time an emperor went on a journey. The Mughals invariably travelled in utmost luxury, either carried in a litter or riding in an elaborate howdah on the back of an elephant. They were accompanied by hundreds of bearers, elephants, camels and carts. The tent reserved for the emperor's personal use was made of chintz, richly decorated with fringes of silk or satin. The ladies of the court were catered for in much the same manner, riding in litters decorated with gilt and covered by silk nets.[4]

Despite this stunning outward show, the might of the Mughals was not quite as overwhelming as they made it appear. Nor did the imperial writ run throughout India without cooperation from semi-independent local rulers.[5] Throughout his vast domains, the Mughal emperor was effectively in partnership with governors, the *zamindars* or landowners who controlled fortified towns and villages, and salaried officials who gathered the revenues that fed the lavish imperial lifestyle. The system worked well as long as the emperor lived up to the ideal of active, energetic kingship as outlined in the *Arthashastra*. Unfortunately, the line of able Mughal rulers ran out in 1707 when the Emperor Aurangzeb died. There followed a damaging civil war over the succession to the throne and in the resulting anarchy, local tyrants were able to seize power in their own right. New states, large and small, arose with their own rajahs, maharajahs or nawabs and eventually the Mughal emperor was little more than an ornament kept in apparent power for as long as it suited those who had replaced him.

The *coup de grace* was administered by the British who forced the last Mughal emperor, Bahadur Shah Zafar II, to abdicate in 1858 after the suppression of the Indian Mutiny, the last-ditch stand against British rule that began the previous year. Bahadur Shah was subsequently imprisoned.

British dominance in India, which lasted for another ninety years, had effectively begun with the visit of Sir Thomas Roe, ambassador of King James I to the court of the Mughal Emperor Jahangir. Roe, a consummate diplomat with a haughty manner that went down well with the prideful Jahangir, spent four years in India, between 1615 and 1619, and returned home carrying a letter from the emperor that was full of lavish courtesies, which reflected the idea that King James was hallowed in Britain like an eastern potentate. 'Let all people make reverence at your gate,' wrote Jahangir, 'and all monarchies derive their counsel and wisdom from your breast as from a fountain . . .'

More important was the trading monopoly Jahangir granted British merchants, and the freedom they would enjoy to buy, sell, export and travel. British East India Company factors had been in India for almost twenty years by this time, but Jahangir's offer represented the ultimate sanction for their activities. However in 1858, when control of India passed from the East India Company to the British crown, the same practicalities that had once faced the Mughal emperors were still there. The vastness of India, the extreme distance of its more remote areas and the need to use armed force to guard against incursions from neighbouring Afghanistan, made the effective policing of the whole subcontinent difficult, if not impossible.

The British therefore left India's native princes more or less alone to rule their existing states. The princely states occupied a fair proportion of India – around 40 per cent – but of all the European colonisers, the British had the longest continuous experience of monarchy and knew just how potent its influence could be. The princes were generally allowed to rule their states as they wished, but this hands-off policy was not quite as disinterested as it appeared. The princely states were made subject to certain laws that applied throughout British India, such as the abolition in 1829 of *suttee*, the burning of Hindu widows on their husbands' funeral pyres. British education was offered to the rulers' sons and numerous young princes found places at the most highly rated British educational establishments. This had the effect of perpetuating British values and detaching future monarchs from the ruthless despotism of their forebears.

Within the princely states, rulers possessed far greater powers than sovereigns enjoyed under the constitutional monarchy in Britain. Their word was law, their wishes paramount. There was no parliament to dispute power with them. Nevertheless, their days, like those of the Mughals, were numbered. Glory time for the princely states and their rulers came to an end with Indian independence in 1947, although the princes themselves remained some of the richest and most celebrated men in the world. As an acknowledgement of their special position, they were not made subject to the British arrangements for handing over sovereignty. Instead, the rulers had the choice of joining either Hindu India or Muslim Pakistan.

Similarly, in Malaya, the British adopted a system of indirect control while leaving the sultans in place in the various states. This, inevitably, led to the end of the sultans' status as gods. Their divinity and the extreme veneration accorded them was incompatible with the more practical British purposes. Everything about Malay royalty was alien to the British concept of monarchy. In Malay tradition, the sultan was supposed to have white blood in his veins, he possessed supernatural powers and his divinity was confirmed by his impassive behaviour in public and his monopoly of the colour yellow for clothing, hangings and umbrellas. At his installation, the sultan became a new man, and the separation from his old persona was marked by a ceremonial bath. At the same time, the sultan took on a new sanctity and passed this on to his *kebesaran*, the regalia that were the symbols of greatness. Unlike the regalia used at British coronations – the orb or sceptre – the *kebesaran* were not specialised objects, but could consist of musical instruments or weapons. However, once infused with supernatural power, it could mean death for any unauthorised person to handle them. The sultan himself was untouchable, according to the traditional taboo. A special language with its own vocabulary, the *bahasa dalam*, was used inside the sultan's palace to describe his activities.[6]

There were limitations, but only those which placed the sultan high above mundane concerns, on a plane which ordinary mortals could never reach. For example, the sacrosanct sultan did not involve himself in affairs of state. Although imbued with supernatural powers, he did not act as a link between heavenly spirits and the earthly world. His presence alone was thought to presage good luck and prevent bad harvests, famine and disease. There, in passivity, his function began and ended.[7]

The extraordinary riches of Malaya had first brought it to foreign attention almost two thousand years before the British and other Europeans arrived. As early as 100 BC, Indians had known of *Savarnadvipa*, the Land of Gold, and not only of gold but of spices, aromatic woods and other luxuries.

The peak of Malaya's attraction as a rich trading area came in 1403, with the establishment by Muslim traders of the port of Malacca. Ultimately, the Muslim sultans of Malacca came to control the whole west coast of the Malay peninsula but their dominance and that of Malacca itself was relatively brief. The beginning of the end came when the Portuguese arrived in 1511, followed by the Dutch and, much later, by the British. In 1786, the British East India Company established a trading post on the island of Penang. Within thirty years Britain became the sole foreign power in Malaya, after they ousted the Dutch from their colonies and the English adventurers Stamford Raffles and James Brooke acquired Singapore and Sarawak from local rulers. The foothold these acquisitions afforded evolved into active intervention after 1874, when Residents were placed in the various Malay states. In any other context, the intrusion of the British would have diminished royal power as they became the *éminence grise*, the power behind the throne. In the Malay states, however, the British input tended to give the sultans a more positive role. Under the residency system, the sultans agreed to 'take advice' from their Residents in all matters concerning the running of their states, except for custom and religion. Ostensibly, the Resident was there to help sultans improve their administration. What the Residents actually represented was a subtle, hands-off insertion of British interests into the affairs of the Malay peninsula.

In practical terms, as long as the Residents kept within their assigned limits, the system functioned well enough. Some, like Hugh Low, the third Resident in Perak, were of positive benefit to their states. Low commended himself to the Malays, and constructed roads, a railway and a telegraph line for Perak where nothing like these modern innovations had existed before.

However, one of Low's predecessors, J.W.W. Birch, who took up his post in 1874, stirred up serious trouble when he overstepped his brief. Birch was an arrogant, over-zealous reformer. He had a fearful habit of lecturing the sultan of Perak in public and wanted to abolish debt slavery, the system whereby peasants mortgaged themselves to creditors in return for financial assistance. Malay peasants, whose finances were always friable, used the system to raise money, and once their debt was repaid, the mortgage was at an end. This was by no means the same thing as the form of slavery involving actual ownership of human beings which the British had fought to abolish earlier in the nineteenth century. Birch, however, failed to see the difference. As a result, he roused fury and resentment. He compounded his errors by posting public notices announcing Britain's intention to place Perak under direct rule. The Resident's blatant interference aroused so much fury that a group of Malay chiefs assassinated him in 1875.

Eventually, the sultans began to chafe under British control, however indirect, as it occurred to them that the apparent power they were allowed was only a shadow of the real thing. With that, the British found it more politic to boost the power of the sultans and make them symbols of the Malay people. Eventually, when the Federation of Malaya was established in 1948, the sultans provided a pool of sovereignty while still remaining heads of state within their own domains, with control over religion and patronage. Today, Malaysia is a constitutional monarchy, in which the Crown rotates between the various rulers, who sit in council once every five years and elect one of their number as supreme head of state.

Unlike Malaysia and India, Japan was never colonised in the usual way, although American military occupation after the Second World War included many of the same features. One of these was the use of the existing monarch for American purposes. Although the 'divine' Japanese emperor, Hirohito, was strongly suspected of collusion in the aggressions that produced the war in the Pacific, it was also clear that if the American occupiers were going to exert effective control over Japan, they could not do without him. Adolf Hitler could be eliminated, so could Benito Mussolini; Germany and

31

Italy would go on under new political masters, but Japan without Hirohito was inconceivable.

This policy, disagreeable and unjust though it appeared, was intelligently founded. The Japanese had been taught from childhood that their emperor was a god, and that they were *aohitogusa* – growing human weeds – whose task it was to shield him from all danger. He was so holy that looking at him directly was thought to result in blindness. It was even forbidden to pronounce his sacred name: instead, he was referred to as *tenno heika*, 'Lord Son of Heaven'.

Devotion to the emperor meant a willingness to die for him. These ideas had extraordinary effects which both shocked and horrified American soldiers who had to confront the fanatical Japanese fighting methods in the Second World War. In the Code of Bushido, the rule book of the Japanese samurai, defeat was infinitely worse than death, not only an unbearable shame and disgrace, but also a betrayal of the emperor. Either or both were a cause for ritual suicide and there were several instances on the Pacific islands where the Japanese actually asked the victorious Americans for permission to kill themselves.

The kamikaze pilots who deliberately crashed their aircraft on to American ships in 1944 and 1945 provided another instance of this same urge, and so did Japanese soldiers who took part in the suicidal *banzai* charges. Death before dishonour never had a more dramatic impact. The samurai mentality was not, however, confined to the armed forces. It was endemic throughout Japanese society, and defeat in 1945 saw mass suicides among civilians.

These reactions convinced the Americans that disaster would follow if they attempted to treat Hirohito as an ordinary war criminal. Remove him, as many thought he deserved, and put him on trial, as many wanted, and Japanese society could become ungovernable. It was politic, therefore, that Hirohito remain head of state. Stripping him of his divinity was as far as the Americans dared to go.

All the same, it was quite a way to go. Japanese belief in the god-emperor went back well into ancient times, over 2,500 years to around 660 BC, when Jimmu Tenno, descendant of the sun goddess Amaterasu Omikami became the first 'Lord Son of Heaven'. This exalted status did not last all that long, however. Between Jimmu and Hirohito, the 124th 'Son of Heaven', there lay more than a thousand years when the emperor was virtually in abeyance, along with his divinity. By around AD 400, the imperial family had proved itself too weak to impose its authority over the various warring clans. Likewise, the *diamyos*, the powerful landowner warlords, were beyond imperial control and had no compunction about using their private armies of samurai warriors to promote their own ambitions. The imperial appointment of the first shogun, Yoritomo Minamoto, in 1192 was meant to bring order out of chaos. What it actually did was push the emperor even further back into the shadows as the imperial powers were delegated to this new political master and warlord. The emperor and his family disappeared from view, spending most of their time inside the imperial palace. The imperial finances dropped alarmingly as civil war, raging through Japan for years on end, destroyed the estates from which they drew their income. There was so little money that court ceremonies became too expensive to stage. One emperor had to wait nine years before the government could afford his coronation. Many courtiers deserted the court and went to live in the provinces, leaving the emperor in Kyoto with only a few attendants. These attendants were themselves so poor that they had to scratch a living selling verses or antiques in the back streets of Kyoto.[8]

When the palace of the Emperor Go-Tsuchimikado was razed to the ground by fire during the ruinous Onin War of 1467–77, all that could be found as substitute shelter was a badly made building surrounded by a thin bamboo fence, which failed to keep out the rats scavenging through the adjacent city streets. Go-Tsuchimikado died in 1500, but there was no money for a decent coffin and his corpse was left in a storage room. Eventually, after six weeks, Shogun Yoshizumi paid the 1,000 *hiki* necessary to give the emperor a suitable funeral. Go-Tsuchimikado's family was pathetically grateful and granted Yoshizumi a rare privilege – the right to display the imperial chrysanthemum and paulownia crest.[9]

The shoguns were not always that generous. When Go-Tsuchimikado's successor, Go-Kashiwabara, requested funds for his ceremony of enthronement he was turned down. The shogun gave a very tongue-in-cheek explanation for his refusal.

'There is no reason to hold a grand enthronement ceremony,' he wrote. 'If the man being crowned were not worthy to become an emperor, no degree of pomp and splendour would make people revere him. If, on the other hand, he were a worthy man, there is no need of an enthronement ceremony for he would naturally be regarded as the sovereign majesty over the land.'[10]

The emperors were so slightly regarded, so poor, so powerless that they became almost non-persons, even though within the court, elaborate if empty ceremonies went on being performed in their honour. The strict hierarchy of the court nobles was meticulously observed in an atmosphere stiff with traditional etiquette. It was a charade, but even in this atmosphere, the imperial patents that could ennoble a man and give him a position at court were eagerly sought after. When obtained, the recipient ranked higher than the mightiest *daimyo* who had not yet received similar imperial honours.

Japanese life and custom became even more ossified during the two centuries after the Isolation Decree of 1636 closed the island country to foreigners in order to keep out European religious and commercial influences. Meanwhile, the outside world moved on, rapidly developing socially, politically, industrially and technologically, far beyond the scope of Japanese experience. Just how far beyond was clear from the reaction in the city of Yedo when four black *kurofune*, or dragons, belching out smoke, steam and sparks, came sailing into the bay on 8 July 1853 and anchored there. There was panic-stricken uproar. The temples filled with people frantically clapping their hands to make the gods hear their prayers that a *kamikaze*, or divine wind, might arrive to blow the dragons away, together with the 'foreign barbarians' who manned them. Gongs tolled out the warning of impending disaster. Thousands rushed to leave Yedo and took shelter in the surrounding countryside.

The *kurofune* were, in reality, a fleet of four American steamships whose commander, Commodore Matthew Perry, had come to demand that the Japanese end their isolation and conclude a trading treaty with the United States. Behind this request lay the plans of the newly formed Pacific Mail Steamship Company. Japan was situated on the steamship route from San Francisco to Shanghai in China and during their isolation, the Japanese had acquired an evil reputation for mistreating, even killing, foreigners unlucky enough to be shipwrecked on their shores. If a Pacific Mail ship got into difficulties in Japanese waters, the company could not afford to allow its crew or passengers to fall into Japanese hands.

Commodore Perry brought with him a letter from American President Millard Fillmore to the Japanese emperor asking for protection for American seamen who fetched up on the shores of Japan, the right to purchase coal for steamships and the opening up of ports for trade. The Americans also wanted a formal trading treaty. Perry, who was a consummate diplomat, delivered the president's letter with appropriate ceremony, but the Tokugawa Shogun Ieyoshi, who was in power at the time, knew perfectly well that there was an iron fist in the velvet glove. It was evident that the 'barbarians' would not hesitate to open up Japan by force if they had to.

In 1854, Commodore Perry returned to Yedo and concluded a treaty with the shogun on behalf of the American president. Similar trading treaties followed with Britain, also in 1854, Russia in 1855 and the Netherlands in 1855–6. The samurai, whose long-standing power was at risk, staged violent uprisings in protest, but their resistance was futile: the imperial forces, aided by the British, Dutch and Americans were far too strong for them.

Within a short time, though, the urge to resist change and cling to the old ways was overcome by the natural Japanese curiosity over foreign gadgets and inventions. The young Emperor Meiji, who came to the throne in 1867, was himself intrigued by clocks and swords and became a keen collector of autographs. He once wrote to the Pope asking for his autograph: it was provided promptly, by return of post.[11] This fascination with all things western was backed by a revival in the divine powers of the emperor. In February 1868, Meiji abolished the shogunate and announced that he had reclaimed imperial sovereignty and established Japan as a theocracy with himself at its head. This all-embracing nature of divinity was outlined by Prince Hirobumi Ito, principal architect of modernised Japan in his *Commentary on the Constitution*.

> The Sacred throne was established at the time when the heavens and the earth became separated. The emperor is heaven-descended, divine and sacred. He is pre-eminent above all his subjects. He must be reverenced and is inviolable. He has indeed to pay respect to the law, but the law has no power to hold him accountable to it. Not only shall there be no irreverence to the emperor's person, but also he shall not be made a topic of derogatory comment, nor one of discussion.

Meiji was therefore able to command virtually anything and be obeyed without question. The habit of obedience to imperial commands was so deeply ingrained in the Japanese mindset that they quickly made astonishing strides, acquiring elected government, a parliament, modern textile mills, electric light, the cinema, telephone, steamships, a public schools system, a parliament, a new navy trained by the British and an army trained by the Germans. Ultimately, the Japanese rocketed from the medieval to the modern in only forty years, a tenth of the time the same process had taken in Europe.

Meanwhile, in China, the emperor was reaping the bitter fruit of the fate Siam and Japan had so deftly avoided. The first Opium War of 1839–42, which provided such a fearful warning, arose out of British and French attempts to gain a trading foothold in China, and British use of illegal opium imports to force the hand of the Chinese. These much-hated 'foreign barbarians' prised open the entry they desired at the subsequent Treaty of Nanjing: the emperor was obliged to open five 'treaty' ports along the Chinese coast and cede Hong Kong to Britain. Further trading concessions and the opening up of more ports followed the end of the second Opium War of

1856–60, but the consequences were much more serious: the Treaty of Tientsin in 1860 virtually laid the whole of China open to foreign infiltration.

Psychologically, this was a fate worse than death for imperial China which had for centuries regarded itself as infinitely superior to all other countries on Earth. The Chinese emperor, it was believed, held all other nations in thrall and was, in effect, their liege lord, to whom they owed obeisance and tribute.

In 1793, when the English emissary, Lord George Macartney arrived at the imperial Chinese court, he came with a mass of gifts in 600 separate packages. It took 90 wagons, 40 barrows, 200 horses and 3,000 coolies to transport them.[12] The quantity and quality of the gifts pleased the emperor, Quainlong. However, Macartney was astounded to discover that they were treated as tribute from King George III who was himself regarded as one of Quainlong's vassals. The banners decorating the barges that were sent to bring Macartney to the imperial palace read: 'Embassy from the Red barbarians bearing Tribute.' McCartney, not surprisingly, found the Chinese arrogant and uncooperative. When he refused to kowtow to the emperor, the feeling became mutual.

Although Macartney was a diplomat of long experience, Chinese mores seemed to be beyond his ken. He failed to understand that the emperors of China had long ago become accustomed to the most elaborate rituals of respect which amounted to extreme self-abasement on the part of those who came into the imperial presence. The *k'o-t'en* or *kow-tow* was taken as acknowledgement by the persons performing it that they were tributaries of the Son of Heaven. The ritual required visitors to grovel on all fours and hit their foreheads on the ground nine times. This was going too far for Macartney. As a nobleman from a class that controlled English kings through Parliament and never considered them divine, the kowtow was a long way beneath his dignity.

For the Chinese this performance was fully justified as the proper due of a personage who, in their eyes, could not have been more exalted. Nothing less that total submission would do when standing before the occupant of the Dragon Throne which, the

Chinese believed, connected Earth with Heaven. The emperor, as Son of Heaven, was thought to spread his divine aura around the world at sunrise, when he seated himself on his throne. Once, when writing to the Pope, an emperor of China described himself as 'the most powerful of all monarchs on this earth, who sits on the Dragon Seat to expound the word of God'. He also wrote that he was willing to confer on the Pope's niece the supreme honour of becoming one of his concubines. The Pope's response is not known.

The Chinese emperor played a 'divine' role in religion. He officiated at the state sacrifices, where he made offerings to his ancestors, and also presided over the Great Sacrifice, which consisted of nine separate stages. The Chinese deities were 'present', seated on spirit-thrones and the emperor offered them jade, silk, sacrificial food, wine and meat. The emperor was there in full regalia, which he did not remove until the sacrifices had been ritually burned in a furnace.[13]

However, despite their divinity, the power of emperors did not emanate from themselves. The philosopher Confucius taught that they ruled through a mandate from Heaven, which could be bestowed or withdrawn according to an emperor's worth and ability to rule. The displeasure of Heaven, according to Confucius, was indicated by destructive natural phenomena – floods, famine, plague, earthquake or simply unusual weather. All power, all good and all benefit were said to flow from Heaven through the emperor, but he was nevertheless accountable to the gods and had to report them in the Temple of Heaven in Beijing. Here, at the winter solstice, it was the turn of the emperor to prostrate himself before the gods and ask for their blessing on his empire.

It became the custom, too, for emperors to explain themselves to their people in a Valedictory Edict, written in old age towards what was presumably the end of their reign. It was often remarkably frank, even self-deprecating. In 1719, for example, the Emperor Kangxi of the Qing Dynasty wrote this rather depressing personal survey of his 61-year reign, the longest in Chinese imperial history:

I have enjoyed the veneration of my country and the riches of the world; there is no object I do not have, nothing I have not experienced. But now that I have reached old age, I cannot rest easy for a moment. Therefore, I regard the whole country as a worn-out sandal and all riches as mud and sand. If I can die without there being an outbreak of trouble, my desires will be fulfilled.[14]

The perception of the semi-divine emperor, which on the one hand placed him infinitely higher than ordinary mortals, and on the other cast him as a mortal himself, owed a great deal to Confucius. His rules for the personal conduct of the emperor were directed less at an immutable god, more at a fallible human being and were based on a feudal ethic similar to the European concept of *noblesse oblige*; rulers had a duty to be benevolent and just and should avoid the use of force wherever possible. This was not a brief for an absolute ruler, bending his subjects to his inexorable will; nor did it go quite so far as constitutional monarchy, which placed political limitations on rulers. Instead it occupied a philosophical place somewhere in between, while still maintaining the divine connection that made emperors into special beings.

The problem with Confucian theory was that eventually it had an ossifying effect, trapping the emperor and his court into a set-piece existence far removed from the realities of life. Unfortunately, China had no equivalent to the Japanese Prince Ito; like Chulalongkorn of Siam, Ito spent years abroad, studying government, military, political and social systems in other countries and returned home to apply them in his own. Instead, in China intellectual development was stifled, modernising influences failed to penetrate, and the country stewed in its own backwardness until it was too late. As a result, the two Opium Wars sank China into a century of humiliating exploitation.

The Boxer Rebellion of 1900, in which the 'Fists of Righteous Harmony' rose against the 'foreign devils', was an attempt to restore to China and the emperor the respectability they had once possessed. However, in the early years of the twentieth century, a far more powerful imperative was the rise of Nationalist sentiment, led by Dr Sun Yat Sen, which identified the Qing Dynasty as non-Chinese Manchus who had usurped the imperial throne in 1644 and were now ripe for a fall. Since 1895, foreign powers had been cashing in on China's weakness by seizing various territories: the British, for example, appropriated Weihaiwei, the Russians took over the Liaodong peninsula, and the French, who had already occupied Vietnam, settled in Guangdong. There was nothing the Chinese could do to turn back this tide of thievery. Imperial authority barely existed, having lost much of its power with the death in 1908 of the Dowager Empress Cixi. Cixi had been a woman of great cunning and cruelty who had ruled China from 'behind the curtain' for close on fifty years. The imperial administration was deeply corrupt, and was regularly salted of funds by eunuchs and other officials who creamed off their own cut from the moneys passing through their hands. The emperor himself, Pu Yi, was that most vulnerable of creatures, a six-year-old child.

On 30 October 1911, the boy emperor ordered the formation of a new cabinet that was composed entirely of commoners. This was unprecedented. It symbolised the end of Manchu power and more than two thousand years of imperial rule, and the beginning of China as a republic. Pu Yi, no longer a god, no longer an emperor, ended his days in 1967 as a gardener in the People's Republic of China. His fall, from divine monarch to humble labourer, could not have been more spectacular.

# THREE

## *Monarchy and the Church*

Ancient beliefs in the divinity of kings needed adjustment when the idea was adopted by monotheistic religions. Pagan faiths, with their pantheons of deities performing different functions, had been a far more flexible canvas on which to paint kings or emperors as gods in their own right. The 'divine' Roman emperors, for example, simply joined the family of gods. There was no sense of rivalry in such an arrangement and nothing disturbing about newcomers to the club, as it were, joining its long-established members.

In monotheistic religions such as Judaism, Christianity and Islam, there was every reason why this could not happen. In each case, God claimed exclusive rights to faith, and the Old and New Testaments in the Bible issued no less than seventeen separate warnings on the subject. The book of Exodus, for example, was unequivocal.

And God spake all these words, saying, 'I am the Lord thy God, which have brought thee out of the land of Egypt, out of the house of bondage. Thou shalt have no other gods before me. Thou shalt not make unto thee any graven image, or any likeness of any thing that is in heaven above, or that is in the earth beneath, or that is in the water under the earth. Thou shalt not bow down thyself to them, nor serve them: for I the LORD thy God am a jealous God.'[1]

In addition, Christianity could hardly allow kings to rival the position of Jesus Christ, any more than Islam could envisage their intruding on the status of the prophet Mohammed. Ironically, the solution was found in the pagan practices of the Middle Kingdom in ancient Egypt. In this concept, the king was not a god or even the embodiment of God on Earth, but a divine appointee. He was still human but at the same time he was sacred and inviolable, with a God-given right to obedience. An offence offered to a king was an offence against God, and this blasphemy was the ultimate crime, incurring the ultimate punishment.

Confirming the exalted position of monarchs required ceremonies that revealed their connection with God. This was the purpose of the English coronation, which today is the only ritual of its kind still extant among the monarchies of Europe. The coronation of English monarchs consists of an imposing series of rituals that include one supreme moment when God is thought to infuse the new monarch with His spirit. The anointing of a new monarch with holy oil has been traditionally performed in five places on the body: on the hands, chest, between the shoulders, at the elbows and on the head, in a pattern that follows the making of a cross. In addition, a cross is traced on the forehead, again with the holy oil.

Although the anointing marks a threshold which the monarch crosses to become the choice of God, every stage of a coronation has religious meaning. The ceremony is full of religious symbolism which is exemplified by the regalia used. Three swords carried before the sovereign represent Mercy, Spiritual Justice and Temporal Justice, and a fourth, the Great Sword of State, symbolises royal authority. The armills, which are gold bracelets, represent sincerity and wisdom, the orb carried by the monarch represents Christian sovereignty and an indication that the sovereign is supreme head of the English Church. The coronation ring represents royal dignity. There are two sceptres, the Sceptre with the Cross, symbolising the Sovereign's temporal power under Jesus Christ, and the Sceptre with the Dove, which marks the monarch's spiritual role. Together, all this symbolism stands for the enormous weight of obligation loaded on to a monarch and which, it is intended, will be carried for life.

English coronations also comprise a microcosm of the history of monarchy going back to its origins in earliest times. The priestly powers of the sovereign are indicated by the sacerdotal robes worn, and the ritual which dedicates the monarch to the church as one of its servants. The four swords may symbolise civilised virtues, but they also recall the ancient warrior element of the coronation. The acclamation, once marked by knights hammering their swords on their shields, is indicated by the shouts of *'Vivat rex! Vivat! Vivat! Vivat!'* ('The king lives! He lives! He lives! He lives!') At the end of the coronation, members of the aristocracy kneel before the monarch, promising to be his 'Liege man of life and limb and of earthly worship!'[2]

The English coronation ceremony is over a thousand years old and was first devised by St Dunstan, the Archbishop of Canterbury, for the English King Edgar in AD 973. In its essentials, it remained the same at the most recent coronation, that of Queen Elizabeth II in 1953. Dunstan, a thoroughly cosmopolitan man who travelled extensively in Europe, realised that the grand coronations staged for continental kings greatly increased their stature. To put King Edgar on an equal basis, it was necessary for him to have his kingship confirmed by similarly grand rituals.

It was, however, significant that Edgar's coronation was postponed for some years because of his fondness for the high life and the pleasures of the flesh. Dunstan was determined to wait until the king settled down to a more respectable existence. That did not occur until Edgar was thirty, which counted as late middle age at a time when the average expectation of life was comparatively short; wars were frequent and warrior-kings were often cut off in their prime. Edgar, in fact, died only two years after his coronation.

The requirement that kings should be morally spotless, if not saintly, was included in the pre-coronation instructions found in the Hastings collection of manuscripts, on the Ordinances of Chivalry. One of these is a manuscript entitled *The Manner and Form of the Coronation of the Kings and Queens of England 1385–1460*.

The Abbot of Westminster shall for two days before the coronation inform the king and queen of diverse observances that they shall do, warning them also to shrive and to cleanse their consciences before the holy anointing . . .

During the ceremony of coronation, the king had to lie down flat on the pavement before the altar upon cushions and cloths of silk and gold, 'thus arrayed until the Archbishop . . . who shall crown him has said the orison over him'. This procedure was repeated after the monarch took his oath and immediately before the anointing.

The emphasis here was on the monarch as a servant of God, if a very exalted servant, and the humility that must be shown to be worthy of this honour. However, a rather more ostentatious note had already been introduced which had little to do with holiness, but a great deal to do with earthly pride and display. On 16 July 1377, the ten-year-old King Richard II was crowned at the church of St Peter's in Westminster. Monks who saw what happened as the boy king rode to his coronation left behind this sometimes acerbic account:

> . . . they rode towards Westminster through the crowded streets of the city of London, which were so bedecked with cloth of gold and silver, with silken hangings and with other conceits to entertain the onlookers, that you might suppose you were seeing a triumph of the Caesar or ancient Rome in all its grandeur. . . . At the upper end of Cheapside, a castle with four towers had been constructed, from two sides of which wine poured out abundantly. Four beautiful girls . . . dressed in white, stood, one on each of the four towers. As the king approached, they wafted down golden leaves before him, then, as he drew nearer, they scattered imitation golden florins upon him and his horse. . . . At the very top of the castle, which was built up high between the four towers, stood a gilded angel carrying a golden crown; so cleverly was it constructed that it could lean down as the king approached, to present the crown to him . . .

It was, perhaps, unsurprising that Richard II grew up a would-be despot convinced that his word was law and obedience without question was his rightful due. He paid for it first with his throne which he lost in 1399, and the following year with his life. However, though the king as supreme arbiter did not fit into English ideas of the division of power, in Europe there was a great deal to be said for a monarch whose outward splendour and sacred persona struck awe and not a little fear into his subjects. It was an important factor in calming the continent after the chaos that followed the fall of the Roman Empire in around AD 476.

The end of the Roman Empire had removed a long-standing framework of law and order in Europe and let loose the barbarian tribes – Goths, Visigoths, Vandals, Alanni – who preyed on established populations. This era, often called the Dark Ages but more properly termed early medieval, was a period of chronic insecurity with ferocious raiding, destruction and death a constant possibility. Every town, every village was vulnerable, and their inhabitants stood to lose everything in a few terrifying hours of violence and bloodshed – their homes, their cattle, their crops, their families, their lives.

The feudal system provided some defence, organising society into an interlocking series of mutual obligations. It resembled a pyramid, with the king at the apex as the liege lord of the next rank down, the nobility, and the mass of peasants or villeins tied by fealty to the nobles.

This, though, was no substitute for the wide-ranging security, including safety on the roads, which had once been provided by the Roman Empire. Instead, the feudal system established what were basically pockets of local defence, which enabled men of power and ambition to attack the feudal strongholds of other, rival, nobles. Even in England, where royal rule was centralised and strong, and penalties for disloyalty were applied with great brutality, controlling the nobility and curbing the private wars they waged against each other was far from complete.

The Christian Church, by contrast, was an international organisation with adherents in many different European countries and cadres of devout enthusiasts, such as the Irish, who were ready to confront any difficulty and risk any danger in order to bring the word of God to pagan populations. Potentially, therefore, the church was the only organisation likely to restore peace and order by turning rulers away from their heathen practices and establishing Europe as a focus for worship of the one and only true God.

The role of kings in this process was vital and was symbolised on Christmas Day AD 800, when Charlemagne, the Frankish conqueror of a vast empire in western Europe, was crowned Emperor of the West by Pope Leo III in the Basilica of St Peter in Rome. The connotations of this event were immense. Charlemagne – Charles the Great – was presented as the epitome of the Christian prince and defender of the faith against the hordes of pagans who still inhabited Europe. He was regarded, too, as the successor to the Roman Emperor Constantine I who had converted his empire to Christianity after AD 313.

After twenty years and more of conquest, Charlemagne's own empire stretched from the Danube to the English Channel and from the River Ebro in southern Spain to the Baltic Sea. This vast swathe of territory united most of western Europe by AD 804, and on the continent itself, covered a large part of the area once ruled by Rome: it was therefore easy to identify as a successor state of the long-lost Roman Empire.

There were, however, several important differences in the way Charlemagne's empire was publicised. Although it had been created by war, its warlike aspects were largely played down and another emphasis was applied, the emphasis on learning, literature, the arts and the furthering of Christianity through the foundation of monasteries and missionary work among the pagans. The heathen Saxons, for instance, were converted in their thousands, but the legends that built up around Charlemagne made a lot less of the fact that draconian punishments awaited those who refused to cooperate.

Charlemagne was not, of course, the first or the last ruler to have his less salubrious deeds whitewashed from his record, but this had important publicity value at a time when the struggle between Christianity and paganism was an everyday reality. Until 1386, when the last surviving pagan state, Lithuania, turned Christian, warfare had been ongoing for centuries as the pagans fought hard and long to resist infiltration by the new religion. It was understandable, when Christianity demanded complete severance from the ancient past: the abolition of their gods, their ceremonies, their festivals, their sacrifices, everything pagans and their ancestors had known for thousands of years and on which they predicated their lives.[3]

For people accustomed to the flamboyance of paganism in action, worship of a lone, unseen deity, the asceticism of its priests and above all the outlawing of sacrifices added up to a rather pallid exchange. However, the magnificence of kings and emperors chosen to rule by this single God was extremely impressive and better still, tangible. To an extent, these monarchs, the ceremonial that surrounded them, the veneration they attracted and the obedience accorded them made up for the drama the pagans lost when they became Christian.

In this context, Charlemagne was without doubt an awe-inspiring figure and his exploits, as conquering warlord, Christian emperor, lawgiver and educator inevitably found their way into the romantic poems known as the *Chansons de Geste*. These legends extolled his deeds, featured miraculous events connected with his life and painted him as the *beau idéal* of his age.

Charlemagne was a highly suitable subject for this treatment. He was tall, attractive and very much a man's man, with a liking for good food and a healthy libido: he married three times and had three mistresses. His biographer, Einhard the monk, wrote: 'Bodily Charles was well built, strong, and noble in height, measuring seven times his own foot. His head was round, his hair in later years a brilliant white, his expression calm and cheerful, his bearing full of majesty, his tread firm, his posture erect . . .'

As a Christian hero Charlemagne had particular significance. He stood as an example to other kings of the lustre awaiting them if they agreed to set aside their pagan beliefs. Targeting these kings was a very practical way to proceed: convert them and their peoples would follow, since monarchs, and only monarchs, were able to tell their subjects what they must believe.[4]

Needless to say, like all legends – and propaganda – the truth veered quite widely from the fiction. For a start, Charlemagne's relationship with the Church was not as mutually cordial as the tales about him made out. According to his biographer and friend, the monk Einhard, Charlemagne was not at all pleased with a situation in which his empire, which he believed had been sanctioned by God, appeared to have been hijacked by the Pope. Charlemagne's power was already overwhelming – he was both head of state and head of the Church – so that the Pope's attempt to get in on the act was decidedly intrusive. It also marked Charlemagne as the Pope's man and served as a 'hands off' warning to the Empress Irene of Byzantium or a subsequent emperor, with whom he might have wanted to make a diplomatic arrangement of his own.[5]

It appears that Pope Leo III pulled a surprise on Charlemagne at his 'coronation': Christmas Day Mass was just finishing in St Peter's when Pope Leo produced a crown, placed it on Charlemagne's head and pronounced him 'Emperor of the Romans'. Before Charlemagne could react, the congregation was proclaiming: 'To Charles, the most pious Augustus [wise one] crowned by God, and the great and peaceloving Emperor, life and victory!'

Einhard wrote: 'Charles . . . went to Rome . . . and passed the whole winter there. It was then that he received the titles of Emperor and Augustus . . . to which he at first had such an aversion that he declared that he would not have set foot in the Church the day that they were conferred, although it was a great feast-day, if he could have foreseen the design of the Pope.'

It was a *fait accompli* and afterwards there was no escape from the papal connection. However, it appears that Charlemagne made the most of his unexpected elevation: he insisted that his courtiers, bishops and nobles kowtow to him, kneeling down and touching the ground with their foreheads. Charlemagne even required them to kiss his shoe.

It all became academic fourteen years later, when Charlemagne died and his empire disintegrated. Louis, Charlemagne's only surviving son, inherited the empire intact, but afterwards followed Frankish custom and divided it up between his own three sons. These sons further weakened the Empire of the West by squabbling over their inheritance and within a few years the splendid patrimony of Charlemagne had gone. Its glory had depended too much on Charlemagne himself, lacking the permanent institutions, the communications and the ethnic cohesion that might have perpetuated it under subsequent rulers.

The one common term of reference Charlemagne's empire possessed was its Christianity. The part it played in creating a network of Christian kingdoms across Europe helped to establish the Pope in Rome as the greatest of all liege lords, one who could boast monarchs as his vassals. The model vassal in this context was Leo VI, who became emperor of Byzantium in AD 886. Leo, a man of devout asceticism, was the first Byzantine emperor to have the title of 'Pious' inscribed on his coins. He regarded himself as the new Solomon, but also as God's image placed on Earth to be the icon of Christ the King. 'The King,' wrote the commentator Ambrosiaster in the fourth century AD 'possesses the image of God. . . . He is adored on earth as God's vicar.'

Leo's interpretation of his role mirrored his concept of what Christ would do in similar situations. For example, he refused to lead armies into battle: this was a normal duty for Byzantine emperors, but Leo did not think it fitting that Christ, who had died to save the world, should have anything to do with the bloodshed and death of the battlefield. Next, Leo sought to upend the doctrine that Church and state were separate, though complementary: instead, he sought to exert authority over both of them, since both of them came within the purview of Christ.

In his lifetime, Leo's ideas, which he transmitted to his son Constantine VII, were considered peculiar and they certainly ran against mainstream thinking on royal powers and obligations. However, the charitable aspect of their reigns could not be gainsaid: Leo's reign was remarkable for the care he took over the welfare of the poor and the sick, over education, and over mitigating cruel laws and punishments. In following his father's example, Constantine VII was just as meticulous.[6]

From a more worldly point of view, however, the concessions made by Leo and Constantine to the overlordship of Christ were not practical propositions. For other monarchs to emulate them by playing the saint and faithful apostle was to invite exploitation by Popes who could interfere in a kingdom's internal affairs to the point where royal power was undermined. Popes were able to exact a tax called Peter's Pence which was levied for the support of the papacy: the tax started out at one penny per household in the ninth century, but rose steadily as time went on. The Popes were also the final arbiters of justice in the Church courts, which tried cases involving members of the clergy. In both cases, the papal ingredient reduced the power of kings to control their own finances and dispense justice.

The case of King John in thirteenth-century England proved, in particularly dramatic fashion, what could happen when monarchs were not masters in their own realms. In 1205, King John refused to accept Stephen Langton, who had been proposed as Archbishop of Canterbury by the strongminded Pope Innocent III. As a result, Innocent placed England under interdict, a fearful penalty which meant that the country and its people were exiled from the Church and that all religious services except for baptism and dying confessions were forbidden. John took advantage of the situation by plundering Church property in England to the tune of over £100,000. Innocent hit back by excommunicating him. This, in theory, laid John open to attack by any other king who cared to cross the English Channel for the purpose: if that happened – and King Philip II Augustus of France, England's old enemy, was eager to volunteer – Pope Innocent would do nothing to prevent it or protect King John and his kingdom from the assault.

John was eventually forced to give in, and the degree to which he had to abase himself indicated the extent of the power the Pope exerted. Not only did John have to accept Stephen Langton as Archbishop, but he became Innocent's feudal vassal and paid 1,000 marks a year for England and Ireland. It was true that, in exchange for this humbling experience, John enjoyed the Pope's unwavering support and aid during his campaigns in France, where he aimed to retrieve the lost lands of the Angevin Empire formed from the possessions of his parents, King Henry II and Queen Eleanor of Aquitaine. However, papal punch worked out this way only where a king was weak or in an untenable position, like John. Other kings in Europe and England could not be so easily bullied and refused to bend to the papal will. Unlike the Byzantine Emperor Leo VI, most of these monarchs were not saints who saw themselves as reflections of Christ on Earth and therefore the stewards of God, the creator. They were far too worldly for that and far too conscious of the rewards that earthly power could bring. It might have been in the interests of the Church to glorify kings and place them on pedestals, far above the common run of humanity. However, the view these exalted heights afforded fed the royal sense of grandeur while the veneration kings received went to their crowned and anointed heads: in other words, they began to believe their own publicity.

England was a particular battleground in this context. Even before King John, neither the English nor their kings took kindly to the idea of foreign control of any kind and strongly resisted attempts by successive Popes to intrude on English affairs. This was not just an English characteristic: William the Conqueror (William I), a Norman from northern France, and his Archbishop of Canterbury, Lanfranc, who came from Pavia in Italy, shared the same chauvinistic approach. The Pope of the time, Gregory VII, had supported William's invasion of England in 1066 and approved the appointment of Lanfranc, a very distinguished and charismatic churchman. The Pope soon came to regret his enthusiasm. When Gregory demanded that he should be free to exercise papal authority in England and claimed that land converted by St Augustine after AD 597 belonged to the Pope by right, both King William and Lanfranc moved to thwart him. The furthest either king or archbishop would go was to make the condition that royal permission must be obtained before the pope could exercise any power in England.

The Conqueror's two sons, King William II Rufus and King Henry I, quarrelled fiercely with the next Archbishop of Canterbury, St Anselm. Neither William, who succeeded the Conqueror in 1087, nor Henry, who succeeded William II in 1100, would have any truck with Anselm's insistence that obedience to the Pope came before obedience to kings. Their quarrels led both William and Henry to drive Anselm into exile in Europe.

Later in the twelfth century, the greatest and most damaging quarrel between archbishop and king, Church and state, was the dispute that cast King Henry II against his friend Thomas Becket. Theirs was a tragedy of almost Greek proportions, in which neither would give in, neither would compromise. The dispute was ultimately brought to a close by sacrilegious murder. Despite an age gap between them of some fifteen years, King Henry and Becket were long-standing friends. Henry trusted Becket so completely that he made him Chancellor of England soon after he became king in 1154. The reign seemed set fair for a fruitful cooperation between them.

Then, in 1162, King Henry had what he thought was a bright idea. He appointed his friend Archbishop of Canterbury. Becket was already ordained as a priest, but his sudden rise to the highest ecclesiastical post in the land was unprecedented. King Henry wanted an archbishop he could trust to fend off papal demands for a greater say in the affairs of England and this was what he expected Becket to do for him. He could not have been more wrong.

Once Becket became archbishop, a complete change came over him. He immediately resigned as Chancellor. Once he had gloried in the high life and its pleasures, now he abandoned it. Becket gave away his expensive wardrobe, his fine plate and furniture and devoted himself to study, prayer and acts of charity. The fact that Henry's luxury-loving friend had become an ascetic was startling enough, but Becket's conversion went deeper than outward show. Instead of upholding the king's will when it came to dealing with the Pope, he obstructed Henry at every turn. Like Anselm before him, he upheld papal rights over royal rights and a major clash became inevitable.

The moment arrived after the king demanded that clerks found guilty of crimes in the independent church courts should be handed over to the secular courts for punishment. Becket refused even to consider such a thing and his relations with Henry, already strained, turned from friendship to black hatred. Henry hit out at Becket by trumping up various criminal charges against him, including the embezzlement of public funds while he was serving as Chancellor.

However, when Becket appeared in court, dramatically carrying a large cross, he claimed that, as a churchman, the secular judges had no right to try him; he appealed directly to the Pope for aid. Even for Becket, this was going too far. In 1164, realising his life was in danger, he fled to Sens in France.

Becket's exile lasted six years. During that time, the king of France and the Pope managed to patch up a reconciliation between the former friends-turned-enemies. This enabled Becket to return to England on 1 December 1170, but the basic dispute remained unresolved. If anything, it got a great deal worse. Once home, Becket proved even more recklessly defiant than before.

On 14 June 1170, Henry's eldest surviving son, the eight-year-old Prince Henry, had been crowned by the Archbishop of York and became known as the Young King. The crowning of an heir in his father's lifetime was a device designed to spike the guns of powerful rivals and potential usurpers. What King Henry II had forgotten or, more likely, ignored, was the fact that the crowning of monarchs was a long-cherished monopoly of Canterbury. As archbishop, even a disgraced archbishop, Becket's rights had been usurped. He excommunicated the Archbishop of York and the six bishops involved in the Young King's coronation. Although urged to back down, he refused.

Henry was in Normandy for Christmas, and when the news reached him, his famously ferocious temper went into overdrive. Reputedly, he shouted: 'What miserable drones and traitors have I nourished and promoted in my household who let their lord be treated with such shameful contempt by a low-born clerk? Will no one rid me of this meddlesome priest?'

Four of Henry's knights, Hugh de Moreville, William de Tracey, Reginald FitzUrse and Richard le Breton, took this as their cue for action. They crossed to England, arrived at Canterbury and stormed into the cathedral, fully armed. It was around five o'clock on the afternoon of 29 December 1170. The knights found Becket at prayer before the altar and in front of a large, frightened crowd of worshippers, they demanded that he rescind the excommunications. Becket refused.

Close by, a young monk, Edward Grim, was watching from behind the altar. Later, he wrote an account of everything he saw and heard. 'You shall die!' the knights threatened Becket, only to receive the answer: 'I am ready to die for my Lord that in my blood the Church may obtain liberty and peace.'

Then, wrote Edward Grim:

They laid sacrilegious hands on him, pulling and dragging him that they may kill him outside the church, or carry him away a prisoner, as they afterwards confessed. But when he could not be forced away . . . one of them pressed on him and clung to him more closely. Him he pushed off saying 'Touch me not, Reginald; you owe me fealty and subjection! You and your accomplices act like madmen!'

The knight, fired with a terrible rage . . . waved his sword over [Becket's] head. 'No faith,' he cried, 'nor subjection do I owe you against my fealty to my lord the King.'

Then [Becket], seeing the hour at hand which should put an end to this miserable life . . . inclined his neck as one who prays and, joining his hands, he lifted them up and commended his cause and that of the Church to God. . . . Scarce had he said the words than the wicked knight, fearing lest he should be rescued by the people and escape alive, leapt upon him suddenly and with his sword struck him on the head, cutting off the top of the crown. . . . [Becket] received a second blow on the head, but stood firm. At the third blow, he fell on his knees and elbows . . . saying in a low voice: 'For the name of Jesus and the protection of the Church, I am ready to embrace death.'

Then the third knight inflicted a terrible wound as he lay [on the ground] by which the sword was broken against the stones and the crown, which was large, was separated from the head. . . . [Another] knight . . . put his foot on the neck of the priest and, horrible to say, scattered his brain and blood over the stones, calling out to the others: 'Let us away, knights. He will rise no more.'

The 'meddlesome priest', his skull hacked to pieces, his brains spattered on the cathedral floor, was dead, but King Henry was not rid of him. Becket dead became just as irksome for the king as Becket alive. In 1173, Becket was canonised as a martyr. Canterbury became a place of pilgrimage and the cathedral a shrine to the murdered archbishop. The murder outraged Christian Europe, where veneration of Becket became a cult for nearly four centuries afterwards.

Far from being rewarded for their deed, the four knights were disgraced and were forced to do penance by fasting and banishment to the Holy Land. The greatest display of remorse, however, had to come from the king. Soon after the murder, Henry went to Ireland and hid there for a year and more, waiting for the furore to die down. When, eventually, he was forced to return to England, the punishments were serious, but not too damaging, except perhaps to the royal ego. The king was not excommunicated, although he was prohibited from entering a church. In addition, his lands in France were laid under interdict, which meant that the protection of the Church no longer applied there. That laid them open to any rival – most notably the king of France – who cared to invade them. If that happened, Henry would not be able to ask for aid from the Pope. These penalties were withdrawn after Henry met with papal envoys at Avranches in May 1172, but the punishments were still not over.

On 12 July 1174, King Henry, dressed in sackcloth, the traditional garb of humility, walked barefoot through the streets of Canterbury and prayed at the cathedral. He then submitted to a public scourging from eighty monks who beat him with branches. Sore, bleeding and barely covered, the king spent the following night in the freezing crypt where Thomas Becket was buried. Then and only then was Henry given absolution from the sin he had committed.

Some seventeen years earlier, a scandal of almost equal proportions had arisen between Pope Adrian IV and the German emperor, Frederick Barbarossa. The so-called 'Besançon episode' of 1157 was only one in a long line of disputes in which petty annoyances provided an excuse for the clash between Church and state.

On 20 September 1157, Pope Adrian wrote Barbarossa a letter in which the customary pleasantries of diplomatic correspondence barely concealed his fury. Barbarossa, it seems, had neglected to take any action over an attack on Bishop Eskill of Lyons, who was robbed, kidnapped and threatened by 'impious men, the seeds of evil, the sons of crime'.

'Thy serene Highness,' Adrian wrote, 'knows . . . the fame of so great an outrage has already reached the most distant and most unapproachable regions. . . . But thou art said to have hushed this up or rather to have neglected it, that they have no reason to repent of having committed the deed, inasmuch as they already feel that they have gained immunity for the sacrilege which they committed.'

The Pope went on to indulge in a little emotional blackmail, reminding Barbarossa how much he owed the Church, including his imperial crown, and suggesting that 'a perverse man sowing discord' had turned him against his 'most lenient mother, the most holy Roman Church'.

Two distinguished churchmen, the cardinal presbyters of St Clement and St Mark, were sent to Barbarossa to sort the matter out. Barbarossa duly received them at his court in Besançon, but the way he described them showed that he had no intention of cooperating.

'When, on the first day of their coming, we had honourably received them,' Barbarossa declared in a manifesto dated October 1157, 'and on the second, as is the custom, we sat together with our princes to listen to their report, they, as if inflated with the mammon of unrighteousness, out of the height of their pride, from the summit of their arrogance, in the execrable elation of their swelling hearts, did present us a message in the form of an apostolic letter, the tenor of which was that we should always keep it before our mind's eye how the lord pope had conferred upon us the distinction of the imperial crown . . .'

Barbarossa went on to accuse the two cardinals of carrying secret orders and planning to strip the churches of Germany of their treasures: they even carried forms on which to list their ill-gotten acquisitions. Barbarossa sent the two men back to Rome before they could lay hands on anything. This plot was doubtless a piece of fiction, and it was not the real message Barbarossa intended the Pope to receive. The real message was much more fundamental.

> And inasmuch as the kingdom, together with the empire, is ours by the election of the princes from God alone . . . and since the apostle Peter informed the world with this teaching: 'Fear God, Honour the king!', whoever shall say that we received the imperial crown as a benefice from the lord pope, contradicts the divine institutions and the teaching of Peter, and shall be guilty of a lie.

With this, Frederick Barbarossa kicked away the mainstay of the Pope's demand for his obedience. Adrian appealed to the German bishops to bring the recalcitrant emperor back to the 'right' path, but all they could do was to pass on a letter from Barbarossa in which he expressed reverence for the pontiff while standing firm on the 'divine' origin of his imperial appointment.

By this time, the argument had boiled down to a single word: *beneficium*, which the Pope had used to describe Barbarossa's imperial position. Barbarossa interpreted *beneficium* as a fief, or feudal gift and duly took offence at the suggestion that the fief made him a vassal of the Pope. Adrian knew when he was beaten. In February 1158, he wrote a soothing letter giving a less abrasive interpretation of the word *beneficium*: it was *bonum factum*, a blessing or benediction.

This was, in reality, a face-saving exercise on Adrian's part. He had failed to break down Barbarossa's intransigence. The attack on the hapless Bishop Eskill went unavenged. And the Pope had used semantics to sidestep the real issue involved: whose authority was supreme, the Pope's or the emperor's?

The contest was as fresh as ever a century and a half later when King Philip IV of France gave Pope Boniface VIII his own brutal answer to this fundamental question. This was not a war of words, far from it. King Philip took direct action which did not simply defeat the Pope, but destroyed him.

This time, the conflict revolved around a tax levied by Philip on the French clergy, a tax Pope Boniface declared was illegal. Over a period of six years from 1296, Boniface issued papal bulls demanding an end to the tax. Philip ignored the first two, but refused to let the third pass: this was the *Unam Sanctam* issued on 18 November 1302, which stated, *inter alia*, that it was the duty of princes to be subject to the Pope.

This was not a surprising statement from a Pope who had been attended at his coronation in 1295 by kings acting as his acolytes. King Charles II of Naples and his son, Charles Martel, titular king and claimant to the throne of Hungary, had held the reins of Boniface's snow-white horse as he made his way to St John Lateran in Rome. Later, at the coronation feast, the two kings had personally waited on the Pope. Royal authority, the Pope stated in *Unam Sanctam*:

> though it has been given to man and is exercised by man, is not human but rather divine, granted to Peter by a divine word and reaffirmed to him [Peter] and his successors by the One Whom Peter confessed, the Lord saying to Peter himself, 'Whatsoever you shall bind on earth, shall be bound also in Heaven.' Therefore whoever resists this power thus ordained by God, resists the ordinance of God. . . . Furthermore, we declare, we proclaim, we define that it is absolutely necessary for salvation that every human creature be subject to the Roman Pontiff.

Philip IV proved a lot less pliable than the kings of Naples and Hungary and the Pope's unequivocal statement evoked an unequivocal response. King Philip had *Unam Sanctam* publicly burned, and on 7 September 1303, sent 1,300 mercenaries led by Guillaume de Nogaret and Sciarra Colonna to depose Boniface. At the time, Boniface was staying in the town of Anagni, his birthplace, near Rome. The chronicler William of Hundleby described what happened after the force arrived in the town:

> At dawn of the vigil of the Nativity of the Blessed Mary just past, suddenly and unexpectedly, there came upon Anagni a great force

of armed men of the party of the King of France. . . . Arriving at the gates of Anagni and finding them open, they entered the town and at once made an assault upon the palace of the Pope. . . . Sciarra and his forces broke through the doors and windows . . . at a number of points and set fire to them at others, still at last the angered soldiery forced their way to the Pope.

Many of them heaped insults upon his head and threatened him violently, but to them all the Pope answered not so much as a word. And when they pressed him as to whether he would resign the papacy, firmly did he refuse . . . indeed he preferred to lose his head, as he said: '*E le col, e le cape!*' which meant 'Here is my neck and here my head.'

Sciarra Colonna made as if to kill the Pope, but he was held back by some of his men who were loth to go that far. However, the Pope was alone, his retinue and guards having fled, and there was nothing to stop Sciarra's men from pillaging the papal palace. Afterwards, Boniface was taken back to France where he died a few weeks later, poisoned, it was said, on Philip's orders. Four years later, Philip destroyed the Knights Templar by accusing them of magic, sorcery, heresy and sodomy. The trials lasted seven years. The evidence was fuelled by torture, and the end was inevitable: it was the death accorded to heretics – burning at the stake. It was, however, significant that the Templars' prime loyalty was not to their king, but to the Pope.

Pope versus king or emperor therefore had a very long history before the major break came with the Reformation of the sixteenth century. The actual breach was unconnected with the rivalry for supreme power in Europe. However, when Martin Luther made his protest against corrupt church practices at Wittenberg in 1517, he opened the door that enabled some monarchs to make a bid for freedom from irksome papal restraints and enrich themselves in the process. With an eye firmly fixed on appropriating the treasures of the Church, they repudiated the Pope and his jurisdiction, declared themselves Protestant and took kingship in Europe into new and as yet uncharted realms.

# FOUR

## *Renaissance Monarchy*

Martin Luther's 95 Theses of 1517 proved to be the most epoch-making event since the fall of the Roman Empire more than a thousand years before. Luther's protest led to the Reformation and the fundamental split between the Catholic and Protestant Churches. His main argument was that salvation could be earned by faith alone and did not require indulgences – forgiveness of sins – or the purchase of holy relics, which led to fraud, corruption and financial extortion. These were revolutionary arguments, but they were voiced at a time when almost everything else that had underpinned religion in the medieval world was being seriously questioned.

The Catholic Church had largely created the medieval mindset, in which Man was a deeply flawed being living in perpetual fear of divine anger at his sins and in constant need of redemption, which only faith in Christ could supply. The Renaissance, the rebirth of classical learning, which began around 1450 encouraged another, more individualistic way of thinking, and retrieved humans, their talents, their achievements and their future from the shadow of divine control. This was not just an intellectual, artistic or scientific revolution, however. What was also revived was the self-confidence, curiosity and enterprise that had marked the civilisations of ancient Greece and Rome before the chaos of the so-called Dark Ages closed in on Europe.

Not only the ability, but also the right and necessity to question received wisdom, and explore alternative ways of thought became characteristic features of the Renaissance era. This radically shifted the foundations on which the power of the Church was built, for this was a challenge on fronts where its word had once been incontrovertible. Science, medicine, astronomy, geography, cartography, the shape of the earth and the organisation of the heavens were all made subject to new interpretations. Even the nature of God was called into question. Above all, humanism, which gave prime importance to human rather than divine matters, introduced new and startling ideas: that humans were not putty in the hands of God and helpless before His anger and retribution, but possessed the power to decide and direct their own fates and aim for their own goals.

Kings such as Henry VIII of England eagerly grasped the new learning. They patronised great minds, promoted scholarship at their courts and delighted in being termed 'Renaissance men', able to deploy a wide range of abilities and talents. In these circumstances, it was no longer possible for the Church to tout the ideal king as devout, obedient to God and subservient to the Pope. With the Renaissance, kings came of age, becoming celebrities whose fame rested on far more worldly factors – their own charisma, the splendour of their courts, their material wealth and the personal power they exercised over their subjects. God and the pope did not exactly take a back seat in the new scheme of things, but they lost their central position and, for the first time, the Popes had to contend with rivals who had different notions about the precepts of Christianity. What was more, they had the power and the wealth to impose them on their subjects.

One of the most dramatic displays of the new royal prestige took place in 1520 when King Henry VIII of England and King Francis I of France met at the Field of the Cloth of Gold. Francis's purpose was to persuade King Henry to join his side in his rivalry with King Charles I of Spain. In 1519, Charles had beaten Francis in the election for the throne of the Holy Roman Empire but the French king refused to accept second place. He remained at loggerheads with Charles until the end of his reign in 1547. Francis and Henry met several times at the Field of the Cloth of Gold, but no agreement was reached and England and France were at war only two years later. Nevertheless, royal magnificence had rarely been put on such flamboyant public show as it was between 7 and 24 June 1520.

The name of the venue was part of the publicity, since its position between the villages of Guines and Ardres near Calais hardly justified so splendid a title. The village castles were too broken down to be used by the two monarchs, so temporary camps were constructed, one for King Henry at Guines, the other for Francis at Ardres. 'Camps' was something of a misnomer, for they each featured splendid palaces and pavilions, with sumptuous fittings and decorations, separate chapels of great size and a vast hall. Henry's palace, covering one hectare of land, included a gilt fountain with claret and the spiced wine known as hippocras flowing from separate spouts.

Elaborate entertainments were staged – wrestling matches, jousting and shows put on by mummers who performed traditional masked mimes or folk plays. Huge feasts were laid on with mountains of food and wine flowing in abundance. More soberly, Mass was solemnly observed in the chapels, with English and French taking turns at the last of them on 24 June.

At that stage, both King Henry and King Francis were greatly in favour in Rome. Three years previously, they stood by the papacy when it came under attack from Martin Luther. Henry fancied himself as a scholar, when he was in fact little more than a dilettante. He had written a treatise refuting Luther's criticisms and supporting the Catholic Church, however: it earned him the papal title *Fidei Defensor*, Defender of the Faith, in 1521.

Five years earlier, in 1516, King Francis concluded a concordat with Pope Leo X, which ended nearly eighty years of Gallicanism – traditional French resistance to papal authority. Under the concordat, the Pope recovered the right, lost in 1438, to confirm in office those nominees for church appointments – bishoprics, abbacies, priories – who were put forward by the French king. Accord proved only temporary. Gallicanism reasserted itself in 1561 when the papal right restored in the concordat was revoked by the States-General of Orléans. At that time, the principal power in France was Queen Catherine de Medici, who was regent for her ten-year-old son, King Charles IX. Catherine's main aim in life was to preserve the power of the king. The Pope and his demands militated against full royal power, which in France reached its ultimate expression between 1643 and 1715, during the reign of King Louis XIV. Louis, the 'Sun King', was the most absolute of all absolute monarchs. The Pope, of course, had no place in this particularly French scheme of things, and successive holders of the crown of St Peter were excluded from any effective say in the affairs of France until long after the Revolution of 1789.

Despite their attitude towards the Pope and his powers, French kings never seriously contemplated taking their realms out of the papal community. Unlike several other kingdoms, mainly in northern Europe, France never turned officially Protestant, and the French duly persecuted those who embraced the reformed faith. The appalling massacre of Saint Bartholomew's Day in 1572 when hundreds of Huguenots and other French Protestants were murdered was proof enough of attachment to the old religion. So was the assassination, in 1610, of King Henri IV. The assassin, François Revaillac, was a Catholic fanatic who killed the king because of his tolerant attitude towards the Protestants. Protestant rights had been restored by King Henri's Edict of Nantes in 1598, but in 1685 the edict was revoked by King Louis XIV and the Protestant persecutions resumed.

In 1572 and 1685, many Protestant Huguenots who survived the persecutions emigrated to England, where they found that religious affairs had gone the opposite way to those in France. Several European kings and princes, particularly in Germany and Scandinavia, became Protestant for intellectual or spiritual reasons: others broke with Rome after realising that the Reformation meant an independence none of their predecessors had known and the chance to get their hands on rich Church properties. No king, however, broke with Rome and embraced the Protestant faith for more cynical purposes than King Henry VIII when he sought to divorce his first wife, Catherine of Aragon, and marry her nubile lady-in-waiting, Anne Boleyn.

There was nothing unusual about royal divorce in itself. The normal procedure was to apply to the Pope to annul an unsatisfactory marriage and there was rarely any difficulty about it.

Not in Henry's case. The great obstacle in the way of his wishes was Catherine's nephew, Charles I of Spain who was also the Holy Roman Emperor Charles V. Charles, the most powerful monarch in Europe, was the greatest of all champions of the beleaguered Catholic Church. This, though, did not mean that he recognised any sort of papal overlordship. On the contrary, Charles virtually owned the Pope, Clement VII, after he challenged his long-term rival, King Francis I of France, for control of Italy. Charles's forces invaded Italy, defeated the French and captured King Francis in 1525. In 1527, Charles committed the unthinkable: he sacked Rome and held the Pope hostage for several months.

Clement was unable to make a move without Charles's approval, and this was one of the reasons why Henry VIII failed to persuade the Pope to give him a divorce. Charles had no intention of letting the Pope make it easy for Henry to discard his Aunt Catherine and replace her with the upstart Boleyn.

The impasse was broken when Thomas Cranmer, Archbishop of Canterbury, suggested a cunning way out: the king, Cranmer said, should break with Rome, remove and replace the Pope as head of the Church in England, then, as the new Supreme Governor, pronounce his own divorce. There was, however, a price to pay: Henry's marriage to Anne Boleyn, which took place in 1533, was never recognised in Catholic Europe and their daughter, Queen Elizabeth I, was regarded as illegitimate, both personally and as a monarch.

England, meanwhile, was convulsed as the new religion asserted itself. Traditional religious life was dismantled as monasteries and nunneries were dissolved and their properties and treasures reverted to the king. There was fierce Catholic resistance. Many Catholics went underground and followed the old faith in secret rather than give it up. Ordinary folk were seriously confused: many were unable to comprehend or handle fundamental change which in some ways did not look like change at all. The English Church did not become Protestant as Europeans understood the term. King Henry himself was devoted to the Catholic faith, its precepts and its practices: what he imposed on his kingdom was a new religion that retained the outward show and the accoutrements and costume of Catholicism, but did so without the Pope. This 'High Church' factor is still evident in the Protestant Church of England today.

This was one reason why the French Huguenots who sheltered in England from persecution at home were regarded as unusual, even odd. Calvinism, their form of the Protestant faith, was much more ascetic, their religious services much plainer, their everyday dress less subject to flamboyant fashions. Like the Lutherans, a similarly plain people, Calvinists believed that they were going back to the primal excellence of early Christianity, and that colourfully garbed bishops and archbishops and richly decorated places of worship had no place in religious practice.

In Europe, the strongest concentration of this abstemious form of Protestantism was found in Germany, Switzerland and Scandinavia. The Emperor Charles V (Charles I of Spain) strove mightily to expunge it from his territory of the Holy Roman Empire. Germany, where the Reformation had begun, lay at the heart of Charles's empire, which extended over almost all the territory ruled in ancient times by the Romans. Restoring Catholic control over this vast area was, however, impossible even for a monarch of Charles's power and wealth.

The principal difficulty with Germany was that it was not a unified area, but a mass of small states, each with semi-autonomous rulers of their own. The imperial cities of Germany owed allegiance directly to the emperor, but they contained elements with their own commercial and financial muscle in the shape of their prosperous merchants, bankers and industrialists, such as the Fuggers of Augsburg. This family of merchants and bankers had such wealth and influence that no ruler, not even the Holy Roman Emperor, could afford to ignore them. Charles in fact owed the Fuggers his crown as Holy Roman Emperor: in 1519, they had provided him with the money to bribe electors to vote for him rather than for King Francis of France.

The great majority of Germans were peasants, but peasants with what would today be termed 'attitude'. They had emerged from their feudal status of medieval times with political and social ambitions, fuelled by class discontent and resentment against taxes and those lords and princes who exacted them.

To make matters worse, the imperial infrastructure was weak. The Imperial Diet might make decisions, but it was up to the various German states to enforce them. Not all did so, and even those that did often fell short on effectiveness. The lawcourts lacked judicial power. Local feuds and vendettas abounded in the absence of a recognised police force. In addition, many Germans were convinced that the papacy was bleeding them dry financially and that the absence of a sufficiently strong central government meant that extortion from Rome was that much easier. There was, in fact, too much freedom by default in the Holy Roman Empire, which made it difficult for even the emperor to control. New ideas, filtering through into long-established areas of discontent, found the empire fertile ground. German princes were just as susceptible as the humblest peasant. Some of them regarded Martin Luther as one of their own and the Spanish king turned emperor as a devious foreigner in league with the hated papacy.

Of these German princes who preserved Luther by giving him physical protection, by far the most important was Frederick the Wise, Elector of Saxony from 1486 to 1525. Frederick, a notable man of peace who kept Saxony out of all wars throughout his long reign, was opposed to papal power in Germany and came to believe in Luther's principle of salvation through faith. Luther was an innocent man being persecuted for stating the 'truth' and that was enough for Frederick to make maximum efforts to help him.

In 1518, Luther was declared a heretic by Pope Leo X, who formally excommunicated him two years later. Subsequently, the Emperor Charles made Luther an outlaw and after the Diet of Worms in 1521, when Luther refused to recant, Frederick stepped in and more or less kidnapped the controversial priest. He kept Luther hidden in his castle at Wartburg for almost a year. At Wartburg, Luther began translating the Bible into German. This was a very important enterprise in Reformation terms since Luther believed that the Bible was the only true authority in matters of faith. Christians ought to be able to read it for themselves rather than have it read to them and interpreted by priests who, unlike them, were conversant with Latin.

Although Luther did not specifically encourage or lead it, a new religious movement known as Lutheranism arose in Germany and claimed several princes among its adherents. Charles V saw this as royal mutiny and determined to put a stop to it. On 19 November 1530, he issued a decree demanding that the princes abandon their heretical new ideas and return to the Catholic faith. Charles gave them five months, until 15 April 1531, to obey his orders. The princes had no intention of doing as they were told. Instead, led by Landgrave Philip of Hesse and John Frederick, Elector of Saxony, eight princes and representatives from eight German cities met at Shmalkalden in Saxony on 24 December 1530 and formed a league to resist Charles and his demands.

The Schmalkalden League was no mere talking shop. Between them, its members had a formidable army of 10,000 infantry and 2,000 cavalry and fully intended to use them if any one of them was attacked. A formal treaty creating the League was signed on 27 February 1531. Emperor Charles was now in a vulnerable position. Quite apart from the rebel League, he faced other threats from outside: the Muslim Turks were about to make an attempt at conquering Europe and his old enemy, King Francis of France, was still threatening the empire from the west.

The emperor was therefore forced to temporise and bide his time. In 1532, he decreed the Peace of Nuremberg which allowed for toleration of the Lutherans in Germany. Charles had to wait for fifteen years, until 1547, before he was able to challenge the League in battle at Mühlberg and capture its leaders.[1] This, though, was only a temporary victory. Lutheranism and a similar Protestant faith, Calvinism, had put down roots in Germany that could not be destroyed and in 1552, another grouping, the Protestant League, was formed to defend the Lutheran territories.

The ensuing war ended in a most unsatisfactory manner as far as the Emperor Charles was concerned. For over thirty years, his dream had been to lead the Protestants back to the Catholic fold. In 1555, however, he had to admit that this was impossible. At the

Peace of Augsburg on 3 October 1555, a compromise solution was reached based on the principle *cuius regio, eius religio* – to each kingdom its own faith whether Catholic or Lutheran. The following year, Charles, worn out from thirty-seven years of effort and conflict, abdicated as both king of Spain and Holy Roman Emperor.

Augsburg kept the princes of Europe at peace, more or less, for over sixty years, but the time was not yet right for true toleration of religious differences which involved respect for disparate beliefs. The tragedy of the Reformation was that different religious groupings all believed they had got hold of the truth and that all others were heretics. Besides this, the arrangement at Augsburg contained an important flaw. It did not allow toleration of Calvinism, an import from Switzerland, which spread rapidly in Germany. Calvinists eventually became vociferous enough to demand equality with Lutherans and Catholics. Calvinism, which centred on the doctrine of predestination – the principle that future events were ordained by God and were therefore unalterable – claimed two important royal converts: Frederick III, the Elector Palatine, in 1563, and fifty years later, in 1613, John Sigismund, Elector of Brandenburg. However, it introduced a third religious irritant into Germany, by presenting both the Catholics and the Lutherans with another rival. It was because of the Calvinists that the Lutherans of Scandinavia were drawn into the Thirty Years' War, which began in 1618. An immediate cause of the hostilities was the destruction of a Protestant church by the Archbishop of Prague, then the Bohemian capital. The underlying reason was Calvinist fear that their rights were going to be infringed after the Bohemian Diet elected Frederick of Styria, a devout Catholic and a future Holy Roman Emperor, as king of Bohemia. The Calvinists rose in revolt, removed Ferdinand and chose their own, Protestant, monarch, Frederick of the Palatinate. The Calvinists also threw two Catholic members of the Bohemian royal council from a window, an event known as the 'Defenestration of Prague'. The two men fell some 21 metres on to a pile of manure, which caused them minor injuries but major embarrassment.

The Scandinavians became involved in the war after the Calvinists were decisively defeated in 1620 and Catholicism was restored as the religion of the Bohemian state. The three present-day Scandinavian states – Denmark, Norway and Sweden – which had been joined together by the Union of Kalmar in 1397, were the only countries outside Germany to import Lutheranism as a state religion. After the defeat of Bohemia, all of them were in danger from the forces of Catholicism. Sweden had been the first to break with Rome and adopt the Lutheran faith as part of its own fight for freedom from its stronger neighbour, Denmark. Gustavus I Vasa, leader of the fight for independence, was elected king by the Swedish Diet in 1523. He lost no time establishing royal supremacy over the Swedish Church. His reasons were less spiritual, more pragmatic. As first king of a newly independent kingdom, with few resources at his disposal and a hostile and aggressive neighbour, Denmark, Gustavus had many uses for the vast income of the Church: building a strong state, organising a national army, building an efficient navy and promoting trade.

A monarch with an agenda like this could not afford to risk interference from the Pope or, in fact, any outside power. This was why official connections between Sweden and the papacy were severed in 1523. Lutheranism, which had been filtering into the country for some time, was about to become the new state religion, but first Gustavus Vasa had to break the power of the established Church. There was, of course, strong resistance to the royal resolve to make the Church entirely subordinate to the crown. Rather than force the necessary measures through, however, the king resorted to emotional blackmail: he threatened to abdicate if the Diet refused to give him what he wanted. This raised the spectre of renewed union with Denmark and its hated king, Christian II. It was a cunning move on Gustavus's part: however autocratic he might be, the Swedish king was infinitely preferable to the unspeakable Christian, author of one of the worst atrocities of the time, the so-called Bloodbath of Stockholm.

Only seven years had passed since the Bloodbath took place on 8 November 1520, when at least eighty-two guests at a banquet given by King Christian were arrested and executed or drowned. The victims, all of them regarded as enemies by the ruthless king, included two bishops and several Swedish aristocrats, among them

Gustavus's own father. Christian expected that the killings would break the Swedish will to be free of Denmark: it had the reverse effect. The Bloodbath strengthened the Swedes' resolve and in 1527, the thought of losing Gustavus Vasa and once again falling under the power of the terrible Christian was too much for them to contemplate. Rather than that, they gave in to Gustavus's demands.

At the Diet of Vsters in 1527, all Church property was handed over to the king. Church appointments had to have royal approval and the clergy were made subject to the civil law. This last was a fundamental change from previous arrangements, in which the clergy could be tried for crimes only in religious courts under papal jurisdiction. Gustavus's grip on power in Sweden was immensely increased by these measures and his success acted as a way in for the Lutherans whose 'pure word of God' was now to be preached in churches and schools.

Lutheranism did not have a similarly straightforward path in the still unified kingdom of Denmark and Norway, where the new religion was not adopted until 1536. Once again, the change of faith was inaugurated by kings, although the first in the field – Christian II – managed to have feet in both camps. King Christian never contemplated breaking with Rome, and remained a Catholic. Nevertheless, he adopted policies that gradually squeezed out papal influence in his kingdom to the point where Lutheranism was able to take over.

Christian's motive was much the same as Gustavus Vasa's in Sweden, and King Henry VIII's in England: all of them were determined to make themselves master in their own houses. In Denmark–Norway, the Pope might have a residual role, but he was to be a minor player entirely overshadowed by the power of the king. First of all, Christian's legal code did away with appeals to Rome in spiritual cases: instead, the king and his council constituted a court of final appeal. The power of the religious courts and the bishops who ran them was greatly reduced. The clergy was forbidden to acquire land, a move that effectively prevented them from constructing a wealth and power base that might at some time pose a challenge to royal authority.

Understandably enough, all this provoked intense resentment in Denmark, all the more so because in 1521, when Martin Luther became *persona non grata* in Germany, King Christian openly courted the disgraced priest. He invited Luther to come to Denmark and banned the publication of the papal bull excommunicating him. Luther remained in Germany, but his followers were made welcome in Denmark. As far as the Danes were concerned, Christian's attitude towards them piled yet another grudge on to an already bad record, and it is doubtful if the king had time to implement his anti-papal legal code before he was deposed by a cabal of nobles and bishops in Jutland in 1522. Christian planned to raise an army abroad and win back his crown. Instead, in 1532, he was captured by his successor and uncle, King Frederick I, and spent the next twenty-seven years in captivity, until his death in 1559.

Frederick, formerly the Duke of Schleswig-Holstein, had promised at his coronation in 1523 to destroy the Lutheran Church in Denmark. It was a promise he soon broke. Instead of persecuting them, Frederick protected Lutheran preachers and reformers including, most prominently, Hans Tausen, who translated the Old Testament into Danish in 1535.

The Catholic bishops of Denmark were soon protesting loudly, and in 1527 they demanded that Frederick put a stop to the gradual erosion of Catholic practice and influence. In reply, Frederick informed them that no one, Lutheran or otherwise, was going to be forced to renounce his faith, since the king claimed no power over men's souls. Already, in 1526, Frederick had removed from the Pope the right to confirm the appointments of bishops and his refusal to deal with the Lutherans as the bishops wanted was a clear signal that Catholicism in Denmark was finished. Monasteries and Catholic churches were destroyed – all with the permission of the king – and when Frederick died in 1533, he left his throne to his eldest son, Duke Christian, who had been reared as a Lutheran.

The Danish throne was not hereditary but elective, and at this point the council whose task it was to choose the next monarch refused to give Christian the crown. The majority on the council, needless to say, was Catholic.

71

There were no other feasible candidates, though, and the election was postponed. Supporters of the imprisoned Christian II attempted to fill the gap and restore him to his throne. However, their invasion of Denmark set off a civil war that nearly ruined the country before Duke Christian prevailed with aid from King Gustavus Vasa in Sweden.

This was not all Gustavus Vasa did for Duke Christian. He gave him an example to follow. Christian ascended the throne of Denmark in 1537, as King Christian III, and at once demanded much needed funds from the rich Danish bishops. When they refused, Christian had them arrested and thrown into prison. Afterwards, like Gustavus Vasa fourteen years earlier, he appropriated their property and money. One of the bishops died in prison. The rest were eventually released, but were not compensated for their losses nor restored to their former positions. Their places were taken by Lutheran clergymen who were ordained as 'superintendents'.

The ultimate snub to the former bishops and the Catholic Church came at the coronation of Christian III and his German-born queen, Dorothea of Sachsen-Lauenburg, in 1537. Traditionally, the Archbishop of Lund conducted coronations in Denmark. This time, Christian brought in Johann Bugenhagen, a prominent associate of Martin Luther, to do the honours. Bugenhagen afterwards became a professor of theology at Copenhagen University, where a new Protestant faculty was set up to educate the clergy.

Martin Luther himself approved the new church ordinance adopted in Denmark in 1537, and 1550 saw the appearance of a new Bible, in its first-ever Danish translation. By the time Christian III died in 1559, virtually all traces of Denmark's Catholic past had been erased. The Lutheran Church had prevailed not only in Sweden and Denmark, but in the Danish dependencies of Norway and Iceland.

In 1620, however, King Christian IV of Denmark, grandson of Christian III, was faced with a serious crisis as the Catholic forces scored a decisive victory over the Calvinists of Bohemia. The Emperor Ferdinand intended to wipe out all Protestant dissidence within the Holy Roman Empire and restore the Catholic Church to its former position. Although the Scandinavian states had not been part of the empire, there was no guarantee that the Catholic forces would stop at the Danish border. Christian IV therefore decided on a pre-emptive strike into Saxony in 1625. The result was military disaster. The emperor's forces, backed by two renowned leaders, the Austrian General Albrecht von Wallenstein and the Bavarian Johann Tserklaes, Count of Tilly, thrashed Christian's army over and over again until, after four years, the Danish king was forced to sign the Treaty of Lübeck and withdraw from Saxony.

The triumphant emperor now issued the Edict of Restitution, which demanded the return to the Catholics of all Church possessions appropriated by Protestants. Together with the total humiliation of Danish arms, it looked as if it was all over for the Lutherans of Germany as well as Scandinavia. Then, into the breach stepped a charismatic figure: Gustavus I Vasa's grandson, King Gustavus II Adolphus of Sweden, a champion of Protestantism and a shrewd political operator with an eye to expanding his territory into mainland Europe.

In this context, it was in the Swedish interest that the Emperor Ferdinand should not become too powerful, and the Swedes possessed exactly the right instrument to see to it that he did not. Unlike the Danes, the Swedes had the best trained, best equipped and most disciplined army in Europe. Tactically and strategically superb, the Swedish army was a model of military excellence, widely emulated by other countries. Although the Swedes arrived too late to raise the Count of Tilly's siege of Magdeburg in 1630, a rematch the following year saw Gustavus Adolphus triumph in the Battle of Breitenfeld.

From there, Gustavus Adolphus moved into the Rhineland and afterwards, in the spring of 1632, into Bavaria where the Swedes encountered Tilly once again at the Battle of the Lech. Tilly was killed and his army fled, leaving behind most of their baggage and artillery. Now it was Emperor Ferdinand's turn to face serious crisis: the victorious Swedes had penetrated well over 800 kilometres into the heart of his empire and it began to look as if there was no stopping them.

General von Wallenstein, who had been displaced by the Count of Tilly in 1630, was hastily recalled. He scored better success than Tilly, by preventing Gustavus Adolphus from advancing on the emperor's stronghold in Vienna in August 1632. Three months later, Gustavus Adolphus and von Wallenstein faced each other again at Lützen. The Swedes prevailed, but they lost their king: Gustavus Adolphus, aged thirty-eight, was killed in a fierce cavalry engagement. Gustavus's death spelled disaster for the Swedes. Without his energy and inspiration, their army was simply not in the same class, and they were virtually destroyed two years later at the Battle of Nordlingen in Bavaria.

By this time, after seventeen years, the Thirty Years' War was no longer a conflict of religions, but a political contest that finally resolved itself into a struggle between two major European dynasties, the Bourbons of France and the Hapsburgs of Austria and Spain. A new Swedish army linked up with the French in a pact between Lutheran and Catholic that would have been unthinkable at the start of the war. In the confrontations that followed over the next thirteen years, the Hapsburgs came off the worse. They were defeated in one battle after another and along the way, cities, towns and villages were laid waste, entire populations were displaced, and trade and industry declined. The Thirty Years' War proved the most devastating conflict in Europe before the advent of modern weaponry in the nineteenth century. Almost every European state was involved at one time or another, and it took at least two centuries for Germany, the principal battleground, to recover from the devastation.

However, there were winners as well as losers. At the Peace of Westphalia, which ended the war in 1648, the Calvinists were recognised as the equals of Lutherans and Catholics. At Westphalia, the Holy Roman Empire was severely weakened as the Peace recognised the sovereignty of the various German princes. One of them, Frederick William, Elector of Brandenburg acquired so much new territory that he became more powerful than the emperor himself. The Electorate later became the Kingdom of Prussia in 1701, and Prussia, in its turn, carved out a virtual empire in central Europe when the German states were united under Prussian leadership in

1871. The Holy Roman Empire itself had already ceased to exist, in 1806, when it was abolished by Napoleon Bonaparte.

Westphalia afforded the Catholics no joy. As far as they were concerned, the long struggle, intensely damaging and destabilising, had been for nothing. They never retrieved those areas of Germany and Scandinavia lost to the Lutherans. Switzerland, which was recognised as independent of the empire at Westphalia, was claimed by the Calvinists: so was Scotland, where the new religion was known as Presbyterianism. The major victor was France, which became Europe's strongest power after the Thirty Years' War.

By 1648, the Protestant Reformation had fought its last battle and there were no more major wars of religion in Europe. Almost ninety years had passed since the sequence began with the first religious war in France in 1562, but the most obvious result of the Reformation and its conflicts – the fundamental change in the face and faith of Europe – was not the only outcome. Before this, the political basis of European monarchy had always seemed impregnable, even though individual monarchs, particularly in England and France, had been bullied, abused, deposed and even killed by their own subjects. Throughout, monarchy itself had always survived, and its powers – among them the right to dictate religion and its practices – were never seriously questioned by any substantial opposition.

The Reformation, in which two revolutions ran in parallel, changed all that. Just as some kings rejected the Pope and the controls he imposed over them and their realms, so subjects challenged kings and their right to decide their spiritual direction. King Frederick I of Denmark was not merely temporising in 1527 when he told the outraged Catholic bishops that he had no power over men's souls: he had read the runes right, for the time had come for men – and their kings – to make up their own minds about what they believed. If, inconveniently, they chose to embrace the new Protestant faith then, according to Frederick, they had every right to do so. They also had the right to resist attempts by Catholic sovereigns – or Catholic bishops – to force them back into the papal fold.

For the newly Protestant kings, however, removing those powers the Pope had formerly exercised within their realms was not all advantage. Confiscating Church property and seizing Church wealth might give a rosy glow to the royal coffers – and there was a certain elation in being free of Popes who made undue demands and treated kings like feudal vassals – but the papacy also afforded protection for kings in trouble, intervening on their behalf in disputes with other monarchs or their own recalcitrant subjects. Freedom from papal control did not, therefore, come free. Rejecting Rome was like leaving home: the breakaway Protestant monarchs became totally responsible for the preservation and welfare of their kingdoms and had to put up their own defence against enemies, whether at home or abroad.

Handling this new situation required new strategies. One was the Field of the Cloth of Gold syndrome, in which royal power and wealth was put on unabashed display, not as mere ostentation, but to overawe both subjects and enemies with royalty's godlike splendour. These displays were not always public events. Royal courts were the focus for displays of magnificence that found their way into the accounts of foreigners and other visitors. From there, the news reached public notice, performing much the same role as media gossip columns today.

Ironically, pre-Reformation and decidedly Catholic rituals were used for this form of advertising, even at Protestant courts. Lutheranism, for example, was the plainest of plain religions, one that eschewed all outward show, banned expensive accoutrements and made do with unadorned tables for altars. Yet at the Danish court and the court of Brandenburg-Prussia, both of them Lutheran states, Catholic practice was regularly in evidence. Richly decorated canopies were held over the heads of monarchs as they moved about in procession. Bowing and kneeling before the monarch was *de rigueur*.[2]

Monarchs dining in state virtually re-enacted the rituals of the Catholic Mass. The dining table, raised on a dais, covered with a fine linen cloth, with a canopy above, was so arranged that it resembled a communion table. The royal meal began with the king washing his hands, in the same way that priests began and also concluded the consecration at the Mass. The towel on which the king wiped his hands was treated like a sacred relic and was carried away by a gentleman usher who did not fold it over his arm, as was usual, but raised it above his head as if to preserve it from worldly pollution. Once the meal was over and the king had departed, the tablecloth was reverently folded and handed over to a bishop, who genuflected before the table.

Some of the reverence accorded monarchs, including Protestant monarchs, not only derived from the Catholic ceremonies performed at the Eucharist, the ritual re-enactment of Christ's Last Supper, but went far beyond them. It was permitted, for example, for Catholics attending the Eucharist to kneel once before the tabernacle containing the consecrated bread, then turn their backs on leaving.[3] Monarchs, however, were not supposed to see the backs of those they received in audience at court. Visitors were expected to face the monarch for as long as they were in the royal presence, and retire out of the room backwards, bowing and genuflecting all the way.[4]

The religious connotations of royalty that still formed the basis of court behaviour long after the advent of the Reformation harked back to ancient notions of kings as gods. This idea persisted among the monarchies of Asia, and still persists today, though monarchy in Europe never went quite that far. Even so, the idea that kings were, at the very least, special beings, destined by God to rule, and therefore due unquestioning obedience, certainly underlined the way in which monarchs were regarded. This approach suited deeply religious and superstitious times when the mass of subjects were not highly educated, if they were educated at all, and had yet to absorb the principles of Renaissance humanism, which gave Man, rather than God, prime intellectual place in the world. However they were approached and treated, though, monarchs were still human, still subject to flattery and still prone to self-aggrandisement, given the opportunity. And they were given every possible opportunity. Continually exposed to near-slavish deference, surrounded by solemn ritual designed to exalt them, it was hardly surprising if they embraced self-aggrandisement as their natural right. Before the Reformation, papal controls had to some extent curbed the despotic tendencies that went with absolute monarchy. Once the Protestants had got rid of the Pope, however, there was nothing to hold back the untrammelled exercise of royal power, as typified by the despot's most cherished implement, the Divine Right of Kings.

# FIVE

## Absolute Monarchy and the Divine Right of Kings

The supreme example of the Divine Right of Kings and absolute monarchy in action arose in seventeenth- and early eighteenth-century France where, of four successive kings named Louis, three scaled the heights of royal supremacy and the last paid the ultimate price for it. It was therefore fitting that one of the principal handbooks on absolute monarchy was French: Jacques-Benigne Bossuet's famous work on kingship, *Politique tirée des propres paroles de l'Ecriture sainte* (Politics from the Words of Sacred Scripture) was published in 1707. Bossuet was a distinguished French prelate, one of the greatest orators of his day, and was at one time tutor to the dauphin, Louis, grandson of King Louis XIV of France and father of King Louis XV.

Bossuet's presence at the court of Louis XIV was no coincidence. Louis was the epitome of the absolute monarch and Bossuet's book, published towards the end of his immensely long reign of seventy-two years, codified almost every principle by which the king had lived.

Royal power is absolute (Bossuet wrote) . . . the prince need render account of his acts to no one [for] without this absolute authority, [he] could neither do good nor repress evil. It is necessary that his power be such that no one can hope to escape him. . . . The prince, as prince, is not regarded as a private person: he is a public personage, all the state is in him: the will of all the people is included in his . . . you see the image of God in the king and you have the idea of royal majesty. God is holiness itself, goodness itself and power itself. In these things lies the majesty of God. In the image of these things lies the majesty of the prince . . .

79

The great architect of absolute monarchy in France was Armand Jean du Plessis, Cardinal Richelieu. Born in Paris in 1585, Richelieu was the dominant figure in French politics for eighteen years after becoming chief minister to King Louis XIII, in 1624. For Richelieu, absolute royal rule, typified by the Divine Right, was a political strategy, the only strategy which, in his view, could save France from damaging divisions, corruption in high places and royal ineptitude.

This was not a new idea in France: since the reign of King Louis XI who came to the throne in 1461, royal power had been progressively increased, as all authority was gradually centralised on the crown. This was done mainly at the expense of the French magnates. The decentralisation that had obtained in feudal times had suited them well, since it freed them from outside authority on their own territory and enabled them to collect their own taxes. They were also able to dispense justice in their own courts and raise and use their own armies to conduct their own private wars. However, absolute monarchy went a very long way towards curbing the use and abuse of noble freedoms and also took away much of the share in government which magnates had come to regard as their birthright. Gone, too, were the lands, offices, grants of money and other lucrative favours that went with high political status. Instead, the magnates had to stand by as Louis XI replaced them with advisers and officials of humble birth who were frequently raised to the nobility. This newly favoured class was, of course, the sort a king found most easy to control, since their standing relied entirely on his patronage. From 1485, the same system was used by the first Tudor king of England, Henry VII, who provided himself with a new and pliant nobility after the magnates of England had decimated themselves in three decades of civil war.

The French magnates did not, of course, self-destruct like their English counterparts and it was a weakness in the French system that all too often their attachment to the crown had to be bought with royal favours. It was inevitable that these shallow loyalties would disappear once they found themselves short-changed by the king. In 1467, the magnates whose most prestigious leader was

Charles the Bold, Duke of Burgundy, embarked on civil war to put a stop to the reforms of Louis XI and preserve their ancient rights. It took Louis ten dangerous years, until 1477 when Charles the Bold was killed in battle at Nancy, to regain the upper hand and resume laying the groundwork for absolute monarchy in France.

Francis I, who came to the throne in 1515 and was the first king of France to be addressed as 'Your Majesty', was a firm believer in absolute monarchy. Building on Louis XI's policy, Francis targeted the judges who sat in the *parlements*, the principal judicial institutions of France, which included among their functions the right to approve taxes. Francis I, however, had his own ideas about the dispensation of justice. He emasculated the *parlements*, most especially the powerful *parlement* of Paris, forbidding them to interfere in affairs of state, exercise their traditional right of reply to royal pronouncements, or modify royal legislation. New law was, in fact, made in suitably despotic fashion: by means of royal edicts. In 1540, Guillaume Poyet, the Chancellor of France, set out the new parameters for members of the *parlement* of Rouen: 'Once the prince has decreed [his laws], one must proceed; no one has the right to interpret, adjust or diminish them.'[1] The *parlement* was not best pleased with these sentiments: that was evident from the fact that it was afterwards closed down. The Rouen *parlement* was reopened in 1541, but with the king's spies in attendance to keep an eye on its activities.

Absolute monarchy was further refined under Francis's son, King Henri II, who succeeded his father in 1547: tragically, though, the policy received a serious setback when Henri was killed in 1559 while taking part in a tournament to celebrate his daughter's marriage to King Philip II of Spain. Unfortunately, Henri's sudden death and the succession, in turn, of his two weak and sickly sons, Francis II and Charles IX, opened the way for opponents of the crown to make their own bids for power. One was the Protestant Huguenot community, which had been persecuted in the reign of Henry II, the others were the magnates who used the weakness of the crown in a bid to retrieve their lost privileges. The religious wars that ensued lasted for thirty-six punishing years. The way in which they ended in 1598, with the Edict of Nantes, was a triumph for toleration and defeat for the Catholic cause, but it was a setback for the monarchy. The edict gave the Huguenots freedom to worship but absolute monarchy lost much of the ground it had gained since the reign of King Louis XI.

Over a century and a half later, Cardinal Richelieu found it an uphill task to retrieve its former prestige. His first problem was that his king, Louis XIII, was poor material for a glorified, divinely appointed monarch. Louis, who became king of France aged nine after his father, King Henri IV, was assassinated in 1610, was melancholy and diffident by nature. He was a hypochondriac, always examining himself for symptoms and a prey to quack cures. He could also be cruel and cunning and was not above plotting to get rid of those he saw as enemies. He appeared to have no thought for his dynastic duties and persistently neglected his wife, Anne of Austria, whom he married at his mother's behest in 1615. As a result, the marriage was childless for twenty-three years, and the birth of a son, the future Louis XIV, in 1638, was regarded as something of a miracle. This was doubtless why he was named as *dieudonné* – god-given – at his christening. Louis XIII, therefore, was hardly the inspiring, charismatic monarch who could impress himself upon his subjects and his fellow sovereigns. Richelieu realised that only by cloaking this unprepossessing royal in the mantle of absolute monarchy could he hope to raise France's profile to the prestigious heights he had in mind.

The task was made more arduous by the damage done to the name of France since the murder of Henri IV. For the first years of his reign, Louis XIII had been dominated by his mother, Marie de Médicis, who used this power to indulge her rapacious favourites Leonora Dori Galigai and Leonora's husband Concino Concini. Like so many others to reach important positions by this route, the couple enriched themselves by salting the state for properties, privileges and cash. Concini, a Florentine adventurer who was also Queen Marie's lover, ran a much-hated spy system. Ultimately, the corruption led in 1617 to Concini's murder, in which the young king and his favourite Charles d'Albert, Duc de Luynes, were implicated.

There was, too, a trumped up trial where Galigai was accused of witchcraft: found guilty, she was executed.

This distasteful episode at least had the virtue of enabling the sixteen-year-old King Louis to detach himself from his mother. Louis abolished the regency and exiled Marie de Médicis to the provinces. Richelieu, who had been the queen's adviser since 1614, passed from her service to that of her son and in 1624 he was appointed Minister of State. Three years later, he embarked on an uncompromising campaign to impose absolutism on France. For Richelieu, the end justified the means, however violent those means might be. Extreme severity was the watchword, a fact he continually impressed on the reticent King Louis. In the courts even small crimes were heavily punished, on the premise that harsh penalties would discourage worse infringements. Force, repression, even terror became routine as a way of stamping the royal mark on an obedient nation and expunging all protest and resistance. By 1631 Richelieu had brought the magnates to heel, reduced the power of the Huguenots who had set up what was virtually a Protestant state within a state inside France, and provided watchdog officials known as *intendants* in each of the thirty-two new districts into which France was now divided. The last lumber of noble power in feudal times, their castles, were destroyed to prevent their use as power bases. Rivalries between nobles were controlled, or at least toned down, by a ban on duelling.

In each district, the *intendant*, who was answerable only to the monarch, had the right to collect taxes, recruit soldiers and oversee the administration of law and the conduct of trade. They also acted as policemen, ready to detect any sign of local discontent and suppress it before it became dangerous to the royal authority and their own. The work of the *intendants* was backed up by Richelieu's own spy ring which reported dissidents back to the cardinal, and a bevy of pamphleteers who disseminated absolutist propaganda.

However, the mote in the eye of Richelieu's campaign was the Huguenot problem. As a devout Catholic, Richelieu detested the Huguenots. Wiping them off the face of France, if not of the earth, would have suited him very well. He was, however, too shrewd to imagine that he could get away with open persecution, especially after the outrage provoked outside France when an estimated 25,000 Huguenots had been slaughtered in the Massacre of St Bartholomew's Day in 1572.

He was therefore willing, though reluctantly, to tolerate the Huguenots' freedom to worship, as long as they remained loyal to the king and caused no trouble. However, there was nothing supine about the Huguenots and trouble inevitably ensued when they proved unwilling to shrink into a minority practising its faith in enclaves. In 1625, the year after France joined with Sweden in the Thirty Years' War, the Huguenots took advantage of the government's preoccupation to extend their existing power base by capturing the islands of Ré and Oléron. The islands, situated at the entrance to La Rochelle on the Bay of Biscay, were strategically important as seaward defences for La Rochelle, the Huguenot 'capital'.

Richelieu dispatched forces to besiege La Rochelle but he soon found himself hamstrung by the intervention of England on the Huguenots' side. The destruction of the Huguenots as a political force in France was therefore delayed until 1628, when King Louis's forces blockaded them into submission at La Rochelle. The effects of starvation after fifteen months of siege were so appalling that the population of La Rochelle was only 5,000 by the time the blockade ended, a mere fifth of its previous number.

Cardinal Richelieu decided on a publicity coup that would, at the same time, tickle the vanity of King Louis. Despite his perennial 'illnesses', the king loved to play soldier and 'lead' his troops to victory. On 1 November 1628, at Richelieu's suggestion, Louis entered La Rochelle at the head of his army, so advertising the total humbling of the rebellious Huguenots. At the subsequent peace treaty, the Grace of Allais, signed in 1629, the Huguenots retained their religious freedom, but had to dismantle their military organisation and destroy their fortresses.

After his stage-managed entry into La Rochelle, King Louis told the Huguenots: 'I well know that you have done everything in your power to throw off the burden of obedience to me. I forgive your rebellions. If you are my good and faithful subjects, I shall be a good prince to you.'[2] This, though, was not just a piece of *noblesse oblige*.

The French had already had enough of bloodbath wars of religion, and even the hard-nosed Richelieu was unwilling to unleash further Huguenot resistance and further chaos by being too severe in victory.

Cardinal Richelieu died in 1642 and King Louis XIII the following year. Richelieu was succeeded as chief minister by the Italian-born Giulio Mazarini, Cardinal Mazarin, who continued his work on behalf of the new king, Louis XIV. Louis was only five years old when he came to the throne, and between 1648 and 1653 the French nobility and the Parlement of Paris took advantage of his minority: they staged le Fronde, a series of revolts aimed at cutting back the authority of the crown and unseating Mazarin. The uprisings were suppressed. Mazarin survived but on his death in 1661, the now 23-year-old Louis XIV did not appoint a successor: instead, the young king personally assumed supreme power.

Early on the morning of 10 March 1661, the day after Mazarin's death, King Louis summoned Pierre Seguier, his Chancellor, and seven other ministers and secretaries and informed them of the shape of things to come. Louis's ideas were revolutionary. By this time, absolute rule had existed in France for nearly forty years, but personal royal rule, with the king in direct charge of affairs, was as yet unknown.

'. . . up to the present, I have been pleased to leave the government of my affairs to the late Cardinal. It is time for me to govern them myself. You will assist me with your advice when I ask for it. . . . I request and command you, Mr Chancellor, to seal no orders except at my command and without having discussed them with me, unless a secretary of state brings them to you on my behalf. And you, my secretaries of state, I order you to sign nothing, not even a safe conduct or a passport without my command . . .'[3]

The following year, at the Fête de Carrousel, Louis appeared in costume as the sun. With this, he acquired his famous nickname, the *Le Roi Soleil*, the Sun King, but the fancy dress was not meant to be worn, then discarded, after a single evening. Louis was taking on the symbol he believed was most fitting for his status as absolute king.

'I chose to assume the form of the Sun,' he said 'because of the unique quality of the radiance that surrounds it; the light it imparts to the other stars . . . and that constant, invariable course from which it never deviates or diverges – assuredly the most vivid and beautiful image of a great monarch . . .'[4]

King Louis was well aware of the enormous workload he was taking on. His reign was the longest of any European monarch and for more than fifty years during that time, he worked up to nine hours a day. He kept himself 'informed about everything . . . knowing at any time the numbers and quality of my troops and the state of my strongholds, unceasingly giving . . . instructions upon every requirement, dealing directly with ministers from abroad, receiving and reading dispatches, making some of the replies myself, regulating the income and expenditure of my state and keeping my affairs secret as no other man has done before me.'[5]

Secrecy lay at the heart of Louis's method, for he believed that the need to be accountable was not in the best interests of a king. Louis was convinced that it took something away from the magic of rule by Divine Right for a king to have to explain his conduct and, quite possibly, justify it to the public. In an absolute monarchy, subjects had to hear and obey, not agree. Supremely self-disciplined, Louis XIV was able to wear an impenetrable mask whatever his feelings or intentions, and very few people ever managed to penetrate it. However, for his ministers, it was a full-time occupation to keep up with a king who was not the least fazed by the punishing nature of his self-imposed timetable. Nicolas Fouquet, who had been superintendent of finance under Cardinal Mazarin, believed that a life of pleasure would soon lure King Louis away from hard work. It was a complete misjudgment by Fouquet, whose hopes of succeeding Mazarin as chief minister had been foiled by the king in 1661. Louis was perfectly capable of handling with equal gusto his arduous daily work routine, his role as patron of the arts, and the demands of *la dolce vita*, which included producing several illegitimate children by several mistresses. Far from being distracted by his private life, the king thrived on the business of government, and once said: 'I do not know what other pleasure we would not give up for this one . . . I felt an enjoyment difficult to express.'[6]

King Louis had no difficulty in giving concrete expression to the halcyon days of absolute monarchy in France over which he presided. In 1662, he drew up plans for a sumptuous palace at Versailles, 18 kilometres south-west of Paris, which was to serve as tangible evidence of his own glory. Versailles was such a monumental undertaking that some 35,000 work people laboured for twenty years before Louis was able to transfer his court there from the Louvre and Saint-Germain castle in Paris.

Versailles, which had originally been a small hunting lodge built by Louis's father in 1623, became the new seat of government on 6 May 1682. As Louis fully meant it to be, it was the architectural wonder of the age. Its elaborate central block, which took eight years to build, was flanked by two wings, one of them for the royal princes and their wives and children, the other for the courtiers. Beautiful tapestries and furnishings, made by the famous Gobelins factory, adorned the rooms. A separate block accommodated 1,500 servants. There were extensive stables for the master of the horse and his grooms and pages. Special apartments were set aside for the king's mistresses, Madame de Montespan and Madame de Maintenon. Maintenon secretly married King Louis in 1685 after the death of his Spanish queen, Maria Theresa.

Customarily termed a château, Versailles was infinitely more than that: it resembled a small town with accommodation for up to 2,000 people, and contained extensive gardens, grottoes, formal terraces, ornamental ponds lined with statues, and no less than 1,500 fountains and a grand canal to supply the water. There were some 700 rooms, 1,250 fireplaces, 67 staircases and more than 728 hectares of parkland, which also contained two separate castles, Le Grand Trianon and Le Petit Trianon. Distances around Versailles were so great that a sedan chair service was laid on to carry courtiers from one place to another.

The centrepiece of all this grandeur was the Hall of Mirrors where foreign ambassadors were received and the chief court entertainments – masques, fetes, gambling parties – took place. The largest of all the rooms in Versailles, the hall was completed in 1684. At the time, mirrors were new technology and their use at Versailles was revolutionary. Measuring 73m in length, 10.5m in width and 12.3m in height, the walls of the Hall of Mirrors were decorated with Corinthian pillars of green marble. On the inner walls, a row of bevelled mirrors, each facing a window, reflected the lawns, terraces and flowerbeds in the gardens outside. The ceiling, painted by Charles le Brun, depicted scenes from Louis's reign, with the king in various triumphal guises: as a victor in war, as the father of his people, patron of the arts, music, science and architecture, even as a laureated Roman emperor.

This was one of the means by which the French nobility, who were in regular attendance on King Louis at Versailles, were reminded of his God-given powers. Every minute of their intensely busy days was fully taken up with court ceremonial and the demands of strict etiquette. Louis kept his nobles in order not by threats or punishment but by trivialising them. He had never forgotten the terrors of the Fronde which began when he was an impressionable ten-year-old and ended when he was fifteen. The move to Versailles had, in fact, been prompted by events in Paris during the Fronde, which gave Louis frightening memories of the threat the rebellious nobles had posed and the rabid nature of the mob that supported them.

As a class, the nobles never regained King Louis's trust. Like his fifteenth-century predecessor, Louis XI, he preferred to exclude them from his daily councils and rely on humbler-born appointees of his own choosing. If the nobles played power games at court, the aim was not to gain important political advantage or extra territory, but to make sure by untiring effort that they retained the king's favour.

Selected nobles began their day by attending the royal *levée*, where they helped the king rise from bed and get dressed.[7] The day came to an end with the *petit coucher*, when they were in attendance in the king's bedchamber to help him prepare for sleep. Competition for these honours was intense, even when the task in question was emptying the royal bedpan. The diplomat Jean-Baptiste Primi Visconti, count of San Maiaolo, who was in attendance at Versailles in and around 1673, described the scene at the royal bedtime in his *Mémoires sur la Cour de Louis XIV* (Recollections of the Court of Louis XIV):

Prehistoric cave paintings, like this one at Lascaux, were possibly part of religious rites aimed at ensuring a good hunt. *(Ancient Art and Architecture)*

David plays music to King Saul in an effort to sooth his attacks of deep depression. *(Bridgeman Art Library)*

The famous Judgement of Solomon in which the king decided which of two women claiming a baby was the real mother. *(Bridgeman Art Library)*

Julius Caesar, Roman military genius and great-uncle of the first Roman 'emperor', Augustus. *(Bridgeman Art Library)*

Emperor Claudius is shown dressed as Jupiter, the principal god in the Roman pantheon. *(Vatican Museum)*

Maccu Picchu, the fortress deep in the Andes Mountains, was one of a series designed to protect the Inca capital, Cuzco. *(Martin Latham)*

Emperor Mutsuhito, better known as Meiji, headed the government that modernised Japan after 1867. *(Mary Evans Picture Library)*

King Bhumibhol Ayulaydej (left) and Queen Sirikit of Thailand, with Crown Prince Maha Vajiralongkorn in 1999, head a constitutional monarchy first introduced in 1932.
*(PA Photos)*

Emperor Hirohito and Empress Nagako shown in 1926, the year he succeeded to the Japanese throne. Hirohito reigned for sixty-three years.
*(Mary Evans Picture Library)*

The legendary epitome of royal grace and nobility: King Arthur and his knights sit at the famous Round Table. The picture also shows the Holy Grail.
*(Bridgeman Art Library)*

Charlemagne – Charles the Great, King of the Franks and Emperor of the West – shown in his splendid coronation robes.
*(Bridgeman Art Library)*

King Henry VIII was not the jolly 'Bluff King Hal' of legend but, as this picture shows, a terrifying despot. *(Bridgeman Art Library)*

Queen Elizabeth I, the last Tudor monarch, appears in this picture in her coronation robes, orb and sceptre in hand. *(Bridgeman Art Library)*

The magnificent and extensive Palace of Versailles outside Paris typified the might and power of its creator, Louis XIV. *(Bridgeman Art Library)*

The Oath of the Tennis Court (1789) reflected French resolve to have a new, liberal constitution. Revolution followed three weeks later. *(Bridgeman Art Library)*

At his coronation as Emperor in 1804, Napoleon crowned both himself and his wife, the Empress Josephine. *(Bridgeman Art Library)*

The Houses of Parliament in London saw Britain's greatest struggle for power, between the king and Parliament. *(Bridgeman Art Library)*

King Charles I won the Battle of Marston Moor in 1644 (shown here), but lost the English Civil War. *(Bridgeman Art Library)*

Charles I, the only English monarch to be publicly executed, on a freezing cold day in January 1649.
*(Bridgeman Art Library)*

Oliver Cromwell, Lord Protector and chief of the republican government that took power after King Charles's execution.
*(Bridgeman Art Library)*

The English coronation regalia. The republicans sold the regalia after they came to power. A new set had to be made for Charles II.
*(Historic Royal Palaces)*

William III and Mary II, the only married couple to inherit the crown of England as joint monarchs, in 1689. *(Bridgeman Art Library)*

Queen Victoria and Prince Albert are seen here with their nine children, who were born between 1840 and 1857. *(Mary Evans Picture Library)*

The ill-starred Tsar Nicholas II, his wife, the Tsarina Alexandra, and their five children were all murdered by Bolsheviks in 1918. *(Bridgeman Art Library)*

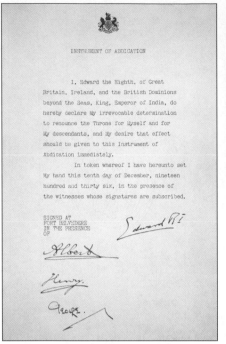

The Instrument of Abdication signed by King Edward VIII in 1936 also shows the signatures of his three brothers. *(Heritage Images)*

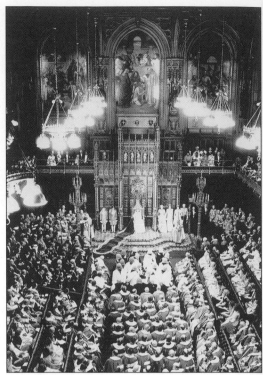

At the State Opening of Parliament, the monarch informs Parliament of the policies that will be followed by the British government, which wrote the speech. *(PA Photos)*

Diana, Princess of Wales, forged a remarkable personal following but her marriage to Prince Charles ended in scandal. *(PA Photos)*

The marriage in 2001 of Crown Prince Haakon of Norway and his bride, Mette-Marit, involved much controversy. *(PA Photos)*

The *petit coucher* is the moment when the King, after disrobing and bidding his courtiers goodnight, has donned his bed robe and is installed on his night-commode. The only persons allowed to be present are those who have the office of Gentleman of the Bedchamber or letters patent which cost as much as 60,000 crowns and which many people would buy for 100,000. (Visconti added, somewhat tongue in cheek:) Thus, you may see what value this nation sets on all that comes from the King, even the most repugnant things . . .[8]

The chance to help the king out of the left arm of his nightshirt, or hand him the nightshirt, was highly prized. These were functions that could be performed only by princes, but others were open to humbler-born officials, especially those with an eye to a noble title. One way to ennoblement was through the post of *porte-coton*: the holder's duty was to hand the king a napkin as he was on his way to the toilet. These tasks, like everything at court, had to be done in the correct order as laid down by etiquette: a mistake, however minor, could mean the withdrawal of royal favour and exile from court.

Attending the royal *toilette* was similarly governed by strict rules. The bowl containing the scented alcohol with which the king washed his face had to be held in a certain prescribed way, and powdering him from head to toe – a performance that occurred several times a day – had to be done with suitable delicacy. Water, thought to be injurious to health, was never used except for a rare bath which doctors might prescribe for health reasons. Louis XIV had only two baths in his entire life of seventy-seven years.

The pressure involved in keeping up with Louis was illustrated by Louis de Rouvroy, Duc de Saint-Simon in his *Parallele des Trois Premiers Rois Bourbons* (Comparison of the First Three Bourbon Kings) written in 1746, some thirty years after the king's death. Saint-Simon was not a neutral observer of the royal scene: he regarded King Louis as a mountainously vain and rather stupid man who deliberately sought out mediocrities to make himself appear more clever. Saint-Simon was an outspoken enemy of absolute monarchy, preferring a nobility that dominated and controlled the king rather than the other way around. Yet, despite these prejudices, even Saint-Simon had to admit to Louis's extraordinary resilience.

'He excelled in all sorts of exercise,' wrote Saint-Simon. '. . . No fatigue nor stress of weather made any impression on that heroic figure and bearing; drenched with rain or snow, pierced with cold, bathed in sweat or covered with dust, he was always the same. . . . I have often observed with admiration that except in the most extreme and exceptional weather, nothing prevented his spending considerable time out of doors every day.'

Getting away from the pressures of court life was virtually impossible unless a courtier was willing to risk losing the pensions and sinecures Louis handed out from time to time as bait. Living at Versailles was a 'must', since it was necessary to be potentially within the royal view at all times. If Louis were to comment that he had not seen one of his courtiers for a while, then that courtier was socially dead.

The reign of King Louis XIV undoubtedly saw the halcyon days of absolute monarchy in France, which under his rule basked in unprecedented lustre as the most prominent power in Europe. The Hapsburgs, the descendants of the Holy Roman Emperor Charles V, had long been dangerous rivals of Louis's House of Bourbon, but they had been put in their place by French victories in the closing phase of the Thirty Years' War. A separate conflict with Hapsburg-ruled Spain ended in another French triumph in 1659. Both wars brought France new territories which gave protection from expansionist Hapsburg ambitions. Inside France itself, Louis exerted a grip on affairs which even the great Richelieu had not been able to manage. Richelieu had identified three major sources of danger to the state and to absolute royal power: the Huguenots, the *parlements* and the nobility. The nobility were, of course, reduced to near puppet status at Versailles, and King Louis was just as ruthless when it came to dealing with the Huguenots. Circumstances had forced Richelieu to tolerate Huguenot religious practices as guaranteed by the Edict of Nantes: King Louis did away with Nantes and in 1685 issued an edict of his own revoking it. This opened the door to renewed persecution and a quarter of a million Huguenots fled into exile abroad. The *parlements*, which had retained a certain amount of latitude in Richelieu's time, found themselves relegated under Louis XIV: he abrogated their right to veto royal legislation and not only that, use of the veto became a crime subject to imprisonment.

Outwardly, the splendours of absolute monarchy and personal royal rule, as exemplified by Louis XIV, represented the dream of all despots come true. However, it had a cardinal weakness: the success and survival of the whole structure relied on the king, or if not the king, then on the presence of a dominant strong man such as Richelieu or Mazarin. If a king were personally suited to rule by Divine Right, with the requisite qualities of leadership, inspiration and the ability to instill fear and respect as well as loyalty in his subjects, then absolute monarchy was a practical proposition. On the other hand, if a king were weak, indecisive, unimpressive or afraid to exploit his 'divine' status then his realm was heading for big trouble.

This, tragically, is what happened to France after Louis XIV's death in 1715. His successors, his great-grandson King Louis XV and Louis XV's grandson, Louis XVI, were mere shadows of their great ancestor, and completely lacked his prestige, political nous and power of command. Louis XV was only five when he came to the throne, three years after a fearful disaster overtook the French royal family. In 1712, an epidemic killed Louis XV's grandfather, both his parents and his elder brother. The two-year-old was saved from death by his nurse: she hid him from the court physicians, whose cures were worse than the disease itself. This tragedy robbed King Louis XIV of the chance to train a successor able to handle the considerable demands of absolute monarchy. These demands became all the more gruelling because Louis XIV had omitted to take note of the obligation which Jacques Bénigne Bossuet expressed like this:

> Kings, although their power comes from on high . . . should not regard themselves as masters of that power to use it at their pleasure . . . they must employ it with fear and self-restraint, as a thing coming from God and of which God will demand an account. . . . Kings should tremble, then, as they use the power God has granted them, and let them think how horrible is the sacrilege if they use for evil a power that comes from God . . .

Too late, on his deathbed, Louis XIV realised how he had used his power for evil, through his costly aggressions against the Dutch and the Spaniards and his expansionist policies that had virtually bankrupted France. Louis had made his France admired for its outward splendour, but also feared for its ambitions. The crunch came in 1701, after King Charles II of Spain bequeathed his throne to King Louis's grandson, Philippe of Anjou. The prospect of a union between the crowns of France and Spain was so alarming that a Grand Alliance of European powers – Britain, the Netherlands, the Holy Roman Empire – declared war. The War of the Spanish Succession lasted twelve years, until 1713, and brought the French spectacular defeats at the hands of Britain's greatest military commander, John Churchill, Duke of Marlborough.

'How could God do this to me after all I have done for Him?' was Louis XIV's reaction in 1704 to the news of Marlborough's victory at Blenheim, one of four great triumphs the duke scored against the French. Eventually, though, the innate arrogance of this statement had given way to regret and guilt for the sufferings France had inflicted on Europe. Louis, in fact, believed that his agonising death from a gangrenous leg was a punishment from God. The future King Louis XV was called to his great-grandfather's bedside.

'My child,' Louis told him, 'you will soon be the king of a great realm. Never forget your obligations towards God: remember that you owe Him all that you are. Try to preserve peace with your neighbours. I have been too fond of war. Do not imitate me in that, nor in the too great expenditures I have made. Lighten the burdens of your people as soon as you can, and do that which I have had the misfortune not to accomplish myself.'

What, if any, impression these words made on the boy, remains unknown, but the reign of Louis XV certainly showed that his great predecessor was wasting his breath. The fifteenth Louis was a popular king, called *Louis le Bien-Aimé* – Louis the Well Beloved – by his subjects, but as an absolute monarch he was a disaster. He never realised that the autocracy he inherited did not exist as a *fait accompli*: to remain effective, it had to be nurtured by constant attention to politics, administration and military affairs. Louis XV lacked his great-grandfather's talents in all these areas. He also developed a distaste for battle brought on during the second Silesian war against Prussia when 7,200 French soldiers under his command became casualties at the Battle of Fontenoy in 1745. Louis XV compounded these weaknesses by allowing his mistress Jeanne Antoine Poisson, the Marquise de Pompadour, an undue influence in both foreign and domestic policy. Pompadour made ministers out of her personal favourites. She largely took over the business of the state, leaving Louis free to enjoy the debaucheries of his personal brothel at 4 rue Méderic, in Stag's Park, an appropriately named district of Versailles.

Louis's reign of almost sixty years was no more than a charade of autocracy. Its foundations and framework were already crumbling by the time he died in 1774 and his grandson, Louis XVI, succeeded to his throne.

Louis XVI's inheritance was crucially weak. Not only was the royal treasury empty but the state was in debt to the tune of £200 million, and though excessive, the levels of taxation could do little to reduce it. The costly French intervention in the American War of Independence, which began in 1775, swelled the national debt even further.

On a personal level, Louis XVI made a bad situation worse still. He was shy, dull-witted, sickly, overweight and indecisive – in no fit state physically or mentally to handle a realm tottering on the edge of disaster. Meanwhile, the grievances of ordinary people in France multiplied as they were weighed down with taxes and denied any say in the government of their own country. Their discontent was encouraged by contemporary ideas that were dangerous to autocracy and to monarchy itself.

Some three centuries after its inception, Renaissance humanism was coming to fruition with notions of popular rights that had not been known in Europe for over eighteen centuries, since the end of the republic of ancient Rome. In 1754, Jean-Jacques Rousseau, the French political philosopher, had published his *Discours sur l'Origine et les Fondements de l'Inégalité parmi les hommes* (Discourse on the Origin and Foundations of Inequality among Men) in which he mounted a fierce attack on private property and argued that human nature, though perfect, was being corrupted by the ills and exploitations of society. Eight years later, in his *Du Contrat Social* (Treatise on the Social Contract) Rousseau suggested that individuals should surrender their rights to the collective 'general will' and, in an evident attack on absolute monarchy, declared this collective to be the sole source of sovereignty.

Rousseau's contemporary, the writer, historian and dramatist Voltaire, whose real name was François Marie Arouet, advocated freedom of thought and belief. Voltaire was himself influenced by the ideas of the English philosopher John Locke, who defended the 'natural' rights and liberty of the individual and the paramountcy of the majority. Neither Rousseau nor Voltaire, both of whom died in 1778, lived to see how their philosophy later convulsed not only France, but Europe. However, they had their successors in the Frenchmen who went to America to help the colonists free themselves from British rule in the War of Independence. In America, men like Marie Joseph Gilbert du Motier, Marquis de Lafayette, who became one of the great heroes of the independence war, were exposed for the first time to freely expressed ideas critical of monarchy which in Europe were tantamount to treason.

The most celebrated critic in this context was Thomas Paine, an Englishman who had emigrated to the United States and took with him a burning hatred of the whole institution of monarchy. In his influential pamphlet *Common Sense*, published in 1776, Paine wrote:

> Male and female are the distinctions of nature, good and bad the distinctions of heaven; but how a race of men came into the world so exalted above the rest, and distinguished like some new species, is worth enquiring into, and whether they are the means of happiness or of misery to mankind. . . . In England a king hath little more to do than to make war and give away places. . . . A pretty business indeed for a man to be allowed eight hundred thousand sterling a year, and worshipped into the bargain! Of more worth is one honest man to society and in the sight of God, than all the crowned ruffians that ever lived.

After the colonists' victory in the War of Independence, Lafayette and his compatriots returned home to France deeply impressed by the willingness of the American colonists to fight and die for their freedom. These were very dangerous ideas in absolutist France. The monarchy came under threat as never before as these influences permeated all classes, from the rich but unenfranchised *bourgeois* to the overtaxed, hungry masses. The traditional *Cahiers de Dolances* (Books of Grievances) first published in 1484, were full of revolutionary demands in the year 1789: a constitution limiting royal power, property rights, individual freedoms, equal rights for all, free speech and an end to the pampering of the nobles who paid no taxes and did no work.

These ideas nullified everything the monarchy had meant in France for over a century and were expressed in horrific violence on 14 July 1789, when an infuriated Parisian mob stormed the Bastille, the symbol of royal repression. Louis XVI had already lost control of events which were powered by the slogan coined by Jean-Jacques Rousseau: *Liberté, Egalité, Fraternité*. On 5 May 1789, at Versailles, he had been forced to summon the Estates General, which represented the three main social classes – clergy, nobles and commons – and, historically, met from time to time to discuss the government of France. This was the first meeting of the Estates General since 1614, and it was like no other.

The demands recorded in the *Cahiers de Dolances* were transferred into action as Louis found himself pressured to reorganise the governance of France along popular lines. At first, he temporised. He tried appeasement, signalling his support for the revolution by wearing its symbol, the red, white and blue cockade. Behind the scenes, however, Louis was plotting to escape with his family, raise support abroad and return to crush the revolution and its protagonists. In March 1791, Louis and his family were apprehended at Varennes while trying to get away. They were taken back to Paris where they became virtual prisoners in their own palace.

On 4 September 1791, now thoroughly terrified, King Louis approved France's first constitution, which transformed him from absolute monarch into powerless figurehead, lacking all his previous powers including the right to declare war and make treaties with foreign countries. The French king was now on a par with the 'constitutional' English monarch who had lost most of his rights and privileges to parliament when constitutional monarchy was introduced a century earlier, in 1689. It soon transpired, though, that the king of England was in a much safer position than his equivalent in France. Constitutional monarchy preserved the English monarch for his role in the new system of government, 'King-in-Parliament'. King Louis had no such safeguard. On 20 June 1792, hardline revolutionaries led by the left-wing Maximilien de Robespierre seized power in the governing Committee of Public Safety. This inaugurated the so-called Reign of Terror in which Robespierre and his supporters went gunning for their class enemies: priests, the nobility, the *bourgeoisie* but first and foremost, the king and his family.

On 21 September 1792, the monarchy was formally abolished in France and four months later Louis XVI was beheaded by guillotine in Paris. His queen, Marie-Antoinette, and other members of the royal family followed. Louis's son, the boy-king Louis XVII became titular monarch of France in prison, and died there in around 1795, possibly by poison. It was, however, ironic that the French Revolution, the most seminal event in modern European history, threw up a leader, Napoleon Bonaparte, who made himself emperor in 1804 and by brilliant military campaigns, spread French power further than even Louis XIV had imagined.

After the final defeat of Napoleon at the Battle of Waterloo in 1815, the Bourbon monarchy was restored in the persons of Louis XVI's brothers, Louis XVIII in 1814 and Charles X in 1824. Louis XVIII, wisely, acknowledged the fundamental changes the Revolution had meant for the monarchy and introduced parliamentary government in France. Charles X, on the other hand, attempted to reimpose the Divine Right and absolute monarchy, only to learn very quickly that France and Europe had not heard the last of the French Revolution.

# SIX

## *1848, Year of Revolutions*

'A successful revolution,' said the Canadian-born economist John Kenneth Galbraith, 'is always the kicking in of a rotten door.'

In France, this was certainly true of the events of 1789, but neither the Revolution nor the return to royal rule after 1814 meant a strengthening of that door. What followed instead was a bitter conflict between oligarchies, royal and otherwise, and the new liberalism. It was a contest played out not only in France, but throughout Europe where the ruling élites and the formerly powerless masses were set on a collision course with a single outcome: the destruction of one and the total triumph of the other. The defining period in this process was the extraordinary year of 1848, when revolutions erupted all over Europe, convulsing the entire political and social structure of the continent. Monarchs who once imagined their privileges were secure and their positions sacrosanct were presented with demands for new constitutions and liberal reforms as the rights of the common people became the watchword of the time. Europe was never the same again and neither was the institution of monarchy.

The French Revolution had drastically changed ideas about the relationship of kings and their realms: once a country had been the personal property of the monarch, now it was possessed by the people who lived there. Like all earthquakes, the upheavals gave out prior warnings even in those countries, like Prussia or Austria, where monarchs had introduced reforms before 1789. This policy, known as 'enlightened absolutism', was a product of the Age of Enlightenment, a philosophical and intellectual revolution that reached its peak in the eighteenth century and advocated social progress, education and the exercise of reason as a means of freeing the masses from ignorance, superstition and exploitation.

'Enlightened absolutism' may sound like a contradiction in terms, but it made sense for those monarchs who realised how it could benefit their realms by giving their subjects something more to work for than squalid living conditions, a pittance for pay and no hope of anything better in the future. Concessions along these lines did not appear to be a danger to royal power. Far from it. In this scenario, the enlightened monarch, demonstrating concern for his subjects' problems, was more likely to earn popular gratitude and at the same time retain his élite position. Voltaire, for one, was sure that the future lay with enlightened absolutism.

In Austria, both the Archduchess Maria Theresa and her son and successor the Emperor Josef II centralised their power along absolutist lines. However, they also embarked on a series of reforms that greatly lightened the burdens borne by Austrian peasants. Of the two, the emperor was the more enterprising. Maria Theresa reduced the incidence of serfdom in Austria, but Josef abolished it altogether. The new liberties Josef subsequently granted to the peasants showed how downtrodden they had been: now they acquired the right to learn skills, to marry, to educate their own children and, generally speaking, to better themselves. The emperor went on to grant extraordinary rights of religious worship. He issued his Toleration Patent in 1781 which emancipated Calvinists, Lutherans and members of the Greek Orthodox church as well as the Jews, who suffered persecution in almost every other European country.

In Russia, which had a very long history of retributive rulers, the Empress Catherine II – Catherine the Great – had read the works of the *philosophes*, such as Voltaire or the radical Denis Diderot, who formulated the ideas of the Enlightenment. She also corresponded with Voltaire in France and, long before she came to the throne, came to the conclusion that Russia was a backward and barbaric country in urgent need of modernisation. More specifically, the country needed to be modernised by means of enlightened absolutism. Catherine came to the Russian throne in 1762 after her insane husband, Tsar Peter III, was deposed and killed, probably with her connivance. Five years later, Catherine issued her *Instruction* outlining policies that were clearly influenced by the advocate of liberty and religious toleration Charles de Secondat, Baron de la Brède et de Montesquieu and by the Italian jurist Cesare, Marchese de Beccaria, whose philosophy took the savagery out of the treatment of criminals. In line with Beccaria's compassion, Catherine abolished judicial torture in criminal trials. She established free schooling in important Russian towns, a degree of religious tolerance, medical services for the poor and needy and introduced the concept of civil rights.

Arguably the greatest of the enlightened despots was Frederick II – Frederick the Great – who came to the throne of Prussia in 1740 and, like Catherine of Russia, absorbed the works of the *philosophes* before he became king. Frederick set down his royal duty in his *Essay on the Forms of Government* in a very high-minded vein.

Rulers should always remind themselves that they are men like the least of their subjects. The sovereign is the foremost judge, general, financier, and minister of his country, not merely for the sake of his prestige. Therefore, he should perform with care the duties connected with these offices. He is merely the principal servant of the State. Hence, he must act with honesty, wisdom, and complete disinterestedness in such a way that he can render an account of his stewardship to the citizens at any moment. . . . Princes, sovereigns, and kings have not been given supreme authority in order to live in luxurious self-indulgence and debauchery. They have not been elevated by their fellow men to enable them to strut about and to insult with their pride the simple-mannered, the poor and the suffering. . . . The sovereign is the representative of his State. He and his people form a single body. Ruler and ruled can be happy only if they are firmly united. The sovereign stands to his people in the same relation in which the head stands to the body. He must use his eyes and his brain for the whole community, and act on its behalf to the common advantage. If we wish to elevate monarchical above republican government, the duty of sovereigns is clear. They must be active, hard-working, upright and honest, and concentrate all their strength upon filling their office worthily.[1]

These sentiments made themselves apparent in Frederick's reforms. He cooperated with representatives of his people in the parliamentary estates. Like Catherine, he followed Cesare Beccaria in eliminating judicial torture. He banned capital punishment. Taking his cue from Voltaire, Frederick protected religious minorities, including Muslims, but excluding Jews whom he taxed heavily in an effort to drive them out of Prussia.

According to the concepts of the Enlightenment, humane reforms, religious toleration and the role of monarchs as servants of the state should have produced a more contented, more fulfilled populace devoted to the rulers whose kindness had improved their lives. It did not happen that way. Individual monarchs, like Maria Theresa or Frederick the Great, were personally admired, but the liberal though despotic premise by which they governed proved unacceptable in the long term. This was not freedom, nor did it represent real human rights: it was a form of patronage that lasted only so long as the monarch was personally committed to the principles of the Enlightenment. Even then, that commitment could not be total if the monarchs in question were also concerned with defending their own position.

King Frederick the Great, for instance, took measures to protect the Prussian peasantry from abuse at the hands of their lords, but still preserved the privileged status of the nobility and retained the institution of serfdom. In Russia, the reforming zeal of Catherine the Great went into reverse when the French Revolution brought home the bloodthirsty extremes to which a nation could go under the impetus of *Liberté, Egalité, Fraternité*. In the Italian state of Tuscany, Leopold II, the grand duke, attempted to give his subjects a liberal constitution which included important restrictions on royal power, only to have it vetoed by his brother, Josef II of Austria.

Likewise, in Sweden, King Gustav III was counted among the ranks of enlightened despots for making public office available to commoners, extending the right of peasants to purchase land and allowing a degree of religious toleration: all the same, he introduced a new constitution in 1772 which increased royal powers and in 1789, for 'security' reasons, introduced new laws that removed the right to legislate from the 'estates' and instead reserved it for the crown.

At best, it seemed, these monarchs were only fair-weather friends of liberal reform. When difficulties arose, they reverted to type and became more despotic than enlightened. A later example of this syndrome was Louis-Philippe, king of France, who was swept to the throne by a liberal revolution in 1830 but thrown off it by another in 1848. Logically, Louis-Philippe, who possessed first-class liberal credentials, should have been a success. He had supported the Revolution, even though his father was guillotined, and in 1793 as a deputy he voted for the execution of his cousin, King Louis XVI. In 1814, Louis-Philippe was a member of the liberal opposition protesting the return of Louis XVIII and the Bourbon monarchy.

Louis-Philippe became candidate for king when Charles X, the last of the Bourbons, refused to accept the majority liberals returned in the elections of 13 July 1830. Charles proceeded to dissolve the new liberal assembly, restrict the vote to big landowners and censure the press. Riots followed, forcing Charles to abdicate. Louis-Philippe, known as the Citizen King, the only sovereign of the so-called July Monarchy, was first elected lieutenant-general of the realm by a provisional government of deputies and peers in Paris. Afterwards, he was proclaimed 'King of the French by the Grace of God and the Will of the People'.

The wording was significant. Louis-Philippe came to the throne as a constitutional monarch committed to a government that limited his powers. He promised to abolish the peerage and extend the franchise, but none of this was possible when he was unable to attract support from a sufficiently wide range of French society. Louis-Philippe relied for his power base on a narrow, though wealthy grouping, the *bourgeoisie*. The extremes of political opinion – the royalists and republicans – were against him. So were the Bonapartists who wanted the return of Napoleon's heirs to the throne of France.

The royalists did not regard Louis-Philippe as royal at all, despite his Bourbon origins. Their 'legitimist' loyalties were with the senior Bourbon line which Louis-Philippe had helped to displace. Besides this, the royalists considered that Louis-Philippe fell short of the gravitas they expected from a king. Royalty, to them, was the awe-inspiring magic of absolute monarchy as it had existed at Versailles during the *ancien régime*. A king, like Louis-Philippe, who walked through the streets of Paris without a guard, wearing an ordinary suit and shaking his subjects by the hand did nothing for the dignity and grandeur of the crown.

As for the republicans and the working class, they did not trust Louis-Philippe to institute the reforms that would improve their economic condition, fully enfranchise them or reduce privilege and equalise society. At the time, France was in deep crisis, financially and industrially. Banks, burdened with debt, were on the edge of collapse. France's major industry, agriculture, was backward and barely existed above subsistence level. A poor harvest was a major disaster, adding to the prevalence of hunger, disease, unemployment and all its attendant ills.

Louis-Philippe barely knew where to begin solving these fundamental problems, and discontent and mistrust were widespread. There were mass protests and demonstrations. Secret republican societies formed, and Louis-Philippe had to face more assassination attempts than any king of France before him. One spectacular attempt to kill him took place in Paris on 28 July 1835. It was the work of a republican named Giuseppe Maria Fieschi who belonged to the extremist Society for the Rights of Man. Fieschi rigged up what the Paris police termed an 'infernal machine' consisting of twenty-five guns with firing pins linked so that they could be let off simultaneously. The result was a fusillade of bullets that killed eighteen onlookers, but left Louis-Philippe and his sons unscathed. Five years later, Louis Napoleon, nephew of Napoleon Bonaparte, made a failed attempt at a *coup d'état* in Boulogne. Meanwhile, Louis-Philippe was under assault from another quarter, as the target of crude cartoons, one of which depicted him as the killer Bluebeard, another as the biblical Cain, the first recorded murderer.

The insults, the contempt, the physical dangers, the sheer impossibility of governing the ungovernable French brought out all

Louis-Philippe's natural autocracy and buried his liberal instincts. He resorted to repression, muzzled the press, and attempted to 'fix' jury trials. Encouraged by his deeply conservative prime minister, François Guizot, he persisently refused to grant any kind of electoral reform. Effectively, Louis-Philippe was reneging on the constitution of 1830: this had brought him to power as 'supreme head of the state, inviolable and sacred' but also guaranteed equality before the law, religious freedom, freedom of speech and other much prized tenets of the liberal creed.

Now the mayhem that was the French political scene in the reign of Louis-Philippe had turned France into a repressive state in which, among other lost freedoms, political meetings were banned. Opposition groups – republicans, radicals, Bonapartists – resorted to subterfuge and found a way to elude the law: they got together at what were, ostensibly, banquets and similar social occasions. The government was not fooled and on 22 February 1848 banned a large banquet due to take place two days later in Paris. Protests and demonstrations rumbled on through the spring of 1848 as large crowds were worked up by extremist republicans and Bonapartists who harangued them on the street corners of Paris.

Under these rabble-rousing influences, the opposition finally blew its fuse. Taking the slogan 'Liberty or Death!' protesters built barricades where they planned to fight it out with government forces, and looted gunsmiths' shops for weapons. Meanwhile, a large mob surged towards the royal palace at the Tuileries which they proceeded to pillage.

Next, they moved on to the Prefecture of Police and the Post Office. Some of them invaded the Chamber of Deputies and later the mob took over the Hotel de Ville, where a republic was proclaimed. In a mood of high, not to say hysterical, excitement, vows were taken to reduce working hours and guarantee jobs for the unemployed.

Meanwhile, Louis-Philippe was making a desperate attempt to save the situation. He sacked the reactionary François Guizot and replaced him as prime minister with the more liberal Louis Mathieu, Comte Molé. It was too late. Revolutionary barricades were already being built – 1,500 of them by 24 February – and the mass insurrection was already under way. Louis-Philippe knew the end when he saw it. He abdicated and got away while he could, fleeing to England in disguise as 'Mr Smith'. He died in exile in Claremont, Surrey, in 1850.

Two decades earlier, the revolution that had brought Louis-Philippe to his throne had set off echoes in the Netherlands, Poland, and some of the Italian and German states. In all these places, grievances were aired with a frightening degree of violence. In Germany, constitutional reforms were granted, but these were withdrawn as the authorities regained the upper hand and suppressed the rebellions. In Poland and Italy, severe repression was used to restore order.

Though limited, the events of 1830–2 turned out to have been a dress rehearsal for the much more widespread and serious revolutions that were inspired by the events in France in February 1848. In Britain the Chartists, who had been agitating for universal male suffrage for some thirty years, said it for all the oppressed of Europe when a meeting in Halifax, Yorkshire, passed a resolution praising the example the French had set. It was, said the Chartists, 'worthy of imitation by all nations crushed beneath the tyrannical sway of Kingcraft, but more especially to those nations governed by a tyrannical oligarchy.'

Ironically, this did not include Britain, where the monarchy had been constitutional for nearly two centuries and the plight of the poor and underprivileged in factories and mines had already been the subject of liberal legislation. Britain, especially London, was not without its tensions[2] and social inequalities of all kinds abounded there. All the same the British, including the Chartists themselves, were generally less revolution-minded than their counterparts in Europe and more inclined to seek redress of grievances through Parliament or by direct appeals to the monarch.

Across the English Channel, however, the Chartist resolution appeared less of a statement, more of a prophecy. Revolution surged across the continent like an epidemic, infecting one country after another. Inspired by the events of February 1848 in Paris, insurrection spread to Austria and Hungary, the myriad states of Germany and Italy, including the Papal States, the Netherlands and Schleswig-Holstein, which was then part of Denmark. Everywhere the symptoms were the same: rejection of absolutist rule, universal suffrage, a free press, trades unions, the right to strike and above all, liberal constitutions. Taken together, the revolutions of 1848 comprised the greatest ever mass assault on the institution of monarchy and all it had stood for.

While popular fury raged, resistance was futile. This time, the revolutions succeeded – or appeared to succeed – not because they were battering at Galbraith's rotten door, but because the reaction of most European monarchs was to take fright, give in and hopefully survive to fight another day. In Prussia, the enlightened absolutism of Frederick the Great had barely outlasted him. In 1788, two years after Frederick's death, his nephew Frederick William II succeeded him and abrogated both freedom of the press and freedom of worship in Prussia. Frederick William's son, Frederick William III, continued Prussia's slide back to authoritarian rule after he came under the influence of Tsar Alexander I of Russia and the Austrian chancellor, Prince Clemens von Metternich. Metternich, who believed in a dominant monarchy backed up by an efficient bureaucracy, was Europe's most prominent exponent of absolute royal rule and his influence on the well-intentioned but impressionable Frederick William was considerable. It led the king to renege on the liberal constitution he had promised. This was greatly to the liking of the monarch's son and successor, Frederick William IV, who became king of Prussia in 1840. The fourth Frederick William had devout attachment to the Divine Right and harboured romantic dreams of a united Christian nation infused with the supposed glories of medieval Germany.

At his accession, he raised hopes of liberal reforms by relaxing press censorship and the setting up of a commission whose members, all representatives of provincial diets, would meet biannually to advise the new king. It soon proved to be a false dawn. Frederick William IV was essentially a conservative ruler with no great love for modern liberal government.[3] In reality, he detested parliaments, constitutions and all the other trappings of popular reform. Above all, he loathed the principles and influence of the French Revolution.

The fallout from that revolution, the uprisings of 1848, reached Prussia in March. Frederick William IV was terrified by the challenge that presented him with danger on his very doorstep. There were vociferous demonstrations in front of the royal palace. The city was gripped by violent disorder for an entire week. Soldiers and citizens fought running battles in the streets of Berlin, the Prussian capital. There were some 200 casualties among the civilians, most of them skilled workers.[4] The bloodshed so infuriated Berliners that Frederick William's brother, Prince William, who led the royalist forces, had to flee abroad and seek shelter in England. He was not able to return to Prussia until the following year.

Meanwhile, Frederick William rapidly caved in, promised a free press with the end of censorship, a meeting of the Prussian United Diet to formulate new electoral laws, a pan-German parliament and a new constitution. His capitulation went so far that it bordered on craven appeasement. In a proclamation entitled 'To My Dear Berliners', Frederick William gave orders for the withdrawal of his troops from the streets and public squares and their return to their barracks and encampments. The commander of the troops in Berlin, General Karl Ludwig von Prittwitz, was incandescent with rage, but he nevertheless followed his orders and the Berlin streets returned to the possession of its citizens.

Von Prittwitz's opinion of the proper royal reaction to rebellion – teaching the upstarts a lesson in brutality they would never forget – was Frederick William's own choice as well. Or it would have been had any real alternative existed in a situation where he was in the hands of the enraged – and dangerous – Berliners. On 21 March, he underlined his submission to the popular will by riding through the streets of his capital wearing the state colours of white, black and gold.

This brought to an end four days of terror and crisis, and Frederick William was able to withdraw to his retreat at Potsdam. He had survived, but the events of 18 to 21 March 1848, which so greatly offended his innate beliefs, left the king in a deeply depressed state. Leopold von Gerlach, an adjutant general, described Frederick William as suffering from a 'mixture of resignation, weakness, apathy and desperation'. His mood was understandable. Like all the conservatives who resisted liberalising reforms both in 1830–2 and in 1848, Frederick William believed that to grant demands was to feed further demands, until the flood of reforms destroyed the established order.

This is what had happened in France after 1789, but 1848 was not going to be like that. There would be no repetition of the escalating violence that culminated at the guillotine in Paris where the royal family and much of the nobility and the *bourgeoisie* were slaughtered in the name of liberty, and the rampant Third Estate recast France in its own bloodstained image. However, for as long as this outcome was possible, the situation appeared grave in the extreme. All the more so because Frederick William's climb-down in Prussia set off a chain reaction of agitation in other German states. An early result was the formation of trades unions which at any other time were anathema to nineteenth-century governments. There was also an attempt to create a united German 'empire' at a nationally elected representative assembly in Frankfurt. The attempt, which was in any case too far in advance of its time, received a setback when King Frederick William IV declined the assembly's offer to become emperor: his reason was that as ruler of Prussia by Divine Right, he could not accept such office from any source other than God. The Frankfurt assembly had a constitutional rather than an absolutist monarchy in mind, and that, doubtless, had its influence on the king's refusal.

Neighbouring Austria endured double trouble, both from its own radicals and the rebels in its twin state, Hungary, who sought to detach themselves from Hapsburg rule. The Hungarian leader, Lajos Kossuth, was a firebrand pamphleteer who had spent time in prison for treason and now called for tax reform and popular representation. The Austrian emperor, Ferdinand, was no match for the eloquent patriot: epileptic, physically deformed and mentally retarded, Ferdinand was totally befuddled by the dangerous situation in which he found himself. He soon yielded to Kossuth and his supporters and on 15 March promulgated laws which gave a large degree of autonomy to the Hungarian government in Budapest.

Two days earlier, a repeat performance of events in Paris had taken placed in Vienna as crowds of demonstrators filled the streets and the troops ordered to disperse them were met with a barrage of stones and other missiles.[5] Before long, the shooting started. Barricades went up. Some of the Civil Guards who were also present refused to obey orders to attack the demonstrators. Disorder and violence escalated. There had to be a scapegoat, and the chancellor and foreign minister, Prince von Metternich, was the ideal candidate. Metternich, who was widely regarded as the real author of imperial repression in Austria, was forced to resign on 13 March. He was replaced by a new prime minister, Prince Felix Schwarzenberg, another conservative but a rather more moderate one.

Ferdinand, meanwhile, was not finished with making concessions. He was obliged to grant freedom of the press, sanction a council of ministers, give his subjects a new constitution and universal suffrage. However, in his fragile mental and physical state, the strain of events proved too much for him. On 17 May he fled from Vienna and took shelter in the archbishop's palace at Olmütz in Moravia. By the end of the year, Schwarzenberg had engineered his abdication, and Ferdinand departed, leaving his throne to his eighteen-year-old nephew, Franz Josef. Afterwards, Ferdinand retired with his wife to Hradschin Castle in Prague where he was no longer an embarrassment to the Hapsburg royal family or an irritant to Schwarzenberg. In retirement, the unfortunate ex-emperor was free at last to follow his hobbies of botany, music and heraldry and indulge in his favourite pastime: cramming himself into a wastepaper basket and rolling round and round on the floor.

The events inside Austria and in Hungary were not, however, the imperial government's only acquaintance with the mayhem of 1848. Austrian territory and interests in Italy also came under threat, this time from agitators who used the year of revolutions to promote a struggle that had already been going on for fifteen years: the unification and independence of Italy, which was the goal of the Young

Italy movement founded in 1833 by Giuseppe Mazzini, a Genovese patriot and republican. The slogan of Young Italy which, unsurprisingly, was very similar to the motto of the French Revolution, was 'Freedom, Equality, Humanity, Independence and Unity'.

By 1848, foreign conquerors had claimed and conquered pieces of Italy for more than 300 years: the Spanish Hapsburgs in the sixteenth and seventeenth centuries, the Austrian Hapsburgs in the eighteenth and, after 1796 and the rise of Napoleon, a French regime that turned the various Italian states into satellites and infused them with the principles of the revolution. This preliminary taste of liberal values was short-lived. With the defeat of Napoleon, the Congress of Vienna, which redrew the map of Europe in 1815, returned Italy to its former despotic masters. Three members of the Hapsburg family received personal legacies. The Grand Duke Ferdinand, uncle of Emperor Franz Josef, received Tuscany; the Archduke Francis d'Este, another Hapsburg prince, was given Modena; and Parma and Piacenza were granted to the Empress Marie-Louise, Franz Josef's daughter and the second wife of Napoleon Bonaparte. The rest of the peninsula was divided between the Pope, who added territory to the existing Papal States; Genoa, which was given the Kingdom of Sardinia; and Ferdinand, son of Charles III of Spain and a descendant of Louis XIV, who received the Kingdom of the Two Sicilies – the island of Sicily and Naples.

This foreign takeover gave rise to protests and violent insurrection which broke out the length of Italy: in Modena, Parma, the Papal States, the Romagna, Ancona, Calabria, and Lombardy. The uprisings were suppressed, but the will to overthrow the foreigners and their despotic rule, especially Austrian Hapsburg rule, was not quenched. In 1837 and 1847 there was disorder, mutiny and attempts to take over the goverment in Naples and Sicily. But it was not until 12 January 1848, six weeks before the uprising against Louis-Philippe in France, that King Ferdinand was faced with the full force of revolutionary fury. He was also threatened with the break-up of his kingdom. Rebels and demonstrators in Palermo, on Sicily, called for a return to the constitution of 1812, which had been formulated under British aegis and included the independence of their island from Naples. Ferdinand called out the troops, but the revolutionaries beat them off, and after holding out for a month the king conceded defeat.

On 10 February, he granted a new constitution which allowed for a chamber of deputies elected by a limited number of voters, but with no restraints on his power and authority and no Sicilian independence. This, of course, was not good enough. The insurrection revived and the barricades went up in Naples. Once again, King Ferdinand gave in, as Sicily proclaimed its own independence, and a revolutionary government set itself up in Calabria.

As the year of revolutions wore on, Italy was overtaken by a ferment of protests and uprisings as similar emergencies threatened a total breakdown of established rule. Even the Pope, Pius IX, was forced to make liberal concessions with his charter of 14 March 1848. When these proved unacceptable – the charter failed to include popular participation in government – Pope Pius fled from Rome. The revolutionaries laid plans to replace papal rule with a republic. So did their counterparts in the constitutional assembly in Tuscany where the grand duke, Leopold II, left Florence in a panic and great haste and joined the Pope in exile in the Neapolitan town of Gaeta.

In the kingdom of Piedmont-Sardinia in northern Italy, a similar struggle took place against the liberal tide, but as elsewhere, the monarch, Charles Albert, was unable to resist the pressure. Royal resistance had lasted only a few weeks before violent agitation in Turin and Genoa, the two main Piedmontese cities, frightened Charles Albert into conceding. On 8 February 1848, with great reluctance, he granted a constitution or *statuto* in which the provisions included religious toleration for non-Catholics and the removal of some restrictions on the press.

However, the *statuto* was not a particularly revolutionary document. Although it provided for a bicameral parliament, both houses were conceived more on conservative than on liberal lines: in the lower house, members were elected by a limited suffrage while in the upper, they were appointed by the king. Parliament shared a certain amount of power with the monarch, although the monarch retained control over important areas such as foreign and military affairs. Parliament had no power, either, over government ministers, who were responsible to the king alone.

Although the most cherished – and fundamental – liberal goals were only partly achieved, the *statuto* was sufficiently acceptable and after it was promulgated on 4 March, the Tuscan politician Cesare Balbo, Conte di Vinadio, presided over Piedmont's first constitutional cabinet. Thus far, the transition from absolute to constitutional monarchy in Piedmont had gone much more smoothly than anywhere else in revolution-torn Europe. Then a serious uprising against the Austrians took place in Lombardy. For five days, ferocious battles were fought in Milan as the people battled with Austrian soldiers for possession of the city. One Milanese, Franco della Pertuta, who kept a daily record of events, described the climax of the struggle as the Austrians, despite desperate resistance, were finally expelled from the city.

With hopes rising of victory in the harsh struggle and of freeing our country from its hated oppressors, spontaneously all families took to decorating the balconies of their houses with the attractive Italian flag. Towards evening the barracks of San Simpliciano were taken back into our possession. With nightfall at about seven-thirty, there could be heard again coming from the Castle the roar of cannon, which went on until past midnight, and with the intermingled and frequent firing of muskets, it was clear that a serious battle was under way. . . . With the dawn came universal rejoicing, and the news soon spread of the victory over our enemies in the night, when a good number of our soldiers had stormed the Castle, striking so much fear into the enemy who realised their desperate condition and decided to retreat. Hastily they had gathered their weapons and kit together with about 300 pieces of artillery, and dragging away with them recruits and Italian soldiers and some citizens whom they were still holding hostage, they left the Castle towards midnight from the Piazza d'Armi and going through Porta Sempione, they fled shamelessly . . .

111

Even the renowned Austrian commander Count Johann Radetzky became part of the humiliating rout. 'It is reported,' wrote della Pertuta, 'that the cruel Radetzky was taken away on a cart, wrapped in a sack of lingerie.' However, although Radetzky, at eighty-two, was well into extreme old age for the time, he had lost none of his masterful cunning. This King Charles Albert discovered after 23 March 1848, when, encouraged by the victory at Milan, he decided to take Piedmont into a full-scale war with Austria.

These were heady days for the supporters of the *Risorgimento*, who imagined their quest for an independent, united Italy was about to transpire. However, the disaster suffered by the Austrians at Milan was not a reliable guide to future events. Charles Albert went to war with much panache, wearing a scarf decorated with the tricolour of free Italy which had been sent to him by the grateful people of Milan. In their excitement, the Milanese mistook Charles Albert's ambitions: he was less concerned with the *Risorgimento*, more occupied with the chance to expand his territory. Nevertheless, in the mood of euphoria that ensued, the king became the symbol of the Italian struggle against tyranny and volunteers flocked to join his army from Lombardy, Naples, the Papal States and Venice.

Disillusionment followed quickly. The Piedmontese army, ill-trained and ill-prepared, were a bunch of amateurs compared to the Austrians, and Charles Albert's military skills were no match for the masterly Radetzky. The volunteers soon fell away and Charles Albert's fate was sealed when he received two severe thrashings, at Custozza and in March 1849, at Novara, where the Piedmontese were routed. This was a severe setback for the *Risorgimento*. Piedmont was forced to return to its original borders of 1815. The humiliation was so great that Charles Albert abdicated his throne and went into exile in Portugal. Within four months, on 29 July 1849, he was dead.

Another twelve years passed before the triad that powered the *Risorgimento* – Giuseppe Mazzini, the visionary, the Piedmontese politician Count Camillo Benso di Cavour and Giuseppe Garibaldi, the military leader – enabled Charles Albert's son and successor, Victor Emmanuel II, to be proclaimed first king of a united Italy on

17 March 1861. Charles Albert's *statuto* was extended to cover the whole of the new kingdom.

This, though, was the only survivor of all the constitutions that were granted under such pressure during the revolutions of 1848, and Piedmont-Sardinia was the only state that retained its constitutional rule. Other reactionary regimes were not down and out, as the revolutionaries may have supposed: they were shocked and knocked off balance, but their apparent collapse and the concessions they had made were not signs of defeat, but of strategic withdrawal. Basically, their absolute power was untouched and, when the time was right, they were able to retrieve their positions.

King Ferdinand of the Two Sicilies exploited his quarrel over the form the oath of allegiance was to take when the moderate assembly elected under the new constitution convened on 15 May 1848. The argument so excited the people of Naples that they began to prepare for battle by putting up barricades in the streets. This was Ferdinand's chance. The same day the assembly was due to meet, firing broke out and the king sent in his troops. They smashed through the barricades, routed the insurgents and within a few hours had Naples under their control.

The Sicilians, meanwhile, were still intent on independence from Naples and rejected Ferdinand's offer of self-government. Instead, they declared him dethroned. That was on 13 April 1848. Four months later, when Ferdinand's rule had been consolidated in Naples, the king set about tackling the Sicilians with some brutality. Between 3 and 7 September, Messina, in the north, was bombarded into submission. After British and French mediation failed to produce an agreement between the warring parties, Ferdinand finished the job and reconquered Sicily by 15 May 1849. Afterwards, the king reimposed his personal rule and the political repression that went with it.

Military repression took care of the revolution in Berlin, where the royalist army returned in force in September 1848. The re-entry of the Austrian army into Vienna cost the lives of 2,000 insurgents out of the 5,000 who had gathered to resist the takeover. In France, where the monarchy had been replaced by a republic, the revolution was hijacked by influential élites, such as the clergy or the affluent *bourgeoisie*. They had plenty of interest in power, but none in social change, especially the kind in which a rampant Third Estate might reproduce the bloody excesses of the Reign of Terror.

The first unmistakable sign that the revolution had been 'betrayed' came in June 1848, when the national workshops in Paris were closed, threatening millions with unemployment and penury. The workshops had been seen as a sign that social change for the better was on the way, and the reaction to their closure was violent. Protesting Parisians once more took to the barricades. The army was ordered in together with the National Guard, and three days of ferocious street fighting followed. A total of 11,642 rebels were arrested, most of them building and factory workers, labourers and navvies, but there were frightful scenes of carnage at the barricades before order was restored.

'When the barricade in the rue de la Mortellerie was taken,' recalled Jean-Louis Meissonier, an artist and a captain in the National Guard, 'I realised all the horror of such warfare. I saw the defenders shot down, hurled out of windows, the ground strewn with corpses, the earth red with blood . . .'[2] Meissonier, who specialised in painting scenes from the Napoleonic wars, later produced a picture of the carnage that was hung in the Louvre in Paris.

Six months later, an ironic tailpiece was written to the year of revolutions when Louis Napoleon was elected president of France with 6 million votes, 70 per cent of those cast. For Louis, this was only the first step towards his real ambition, to emulate his uncle, the great Napoleon Bonaparte, and become emperor of France. The coup that gave Louis the imperial purple he craved took place on 2 December 1851 when the Second Empire was proclaimed and the new emperor took the title of Napoleon III. One of his first acts was to issue a new constitution that made him absolute ruler of France.

These were desolate days for the liberals, radicals and idealists who had hoped for so much from the revolutions of 1848: all the more so because it had appeared, however briefly, that absolute royal power was broken at last and a more egalitarian world was within their grasp. However, the victory of the forces of reaction was not entirely complete. The revolutions had planted the seeds of future democracy in Europe, and although the shoots were small as yet, they would grow with time. Meanwhile, the atmosphere of change was already in the air and the absolute monarchs and their governments never felt entirely safe again. As the nineteenth century progressed, royal families fortified themselves against attack in ways that verged on the psychotic. Black-clad anarchists with sinister beards and smoking bombs may have been figures of fun in newspapers and cartoons, but they were very real and very threatening to their potential targets. Consequently, royals were increasingly smothered in security. They kept themselves more and more apart from their subjects. Wherever unrest arose, they repressed it with the utmost brutality. They employed bodyguards, spies and agents to protect them from assassination. Occasionally, assassins got through the net: there were royal murders in Russia, Greece and at Geneva in Switzerland, where Empress Elisabeth of Austria was killed in 1898. Every time this happened, royal fears grew and the fortress mentality became more intense.

This, though, was not the way to ensure the survival of monarchy and the ruling dynasties. The way to do that was a secret discovered by the British nearly two centuries earlier. Because of it, Britain was one of the few states in Europe to escape the ravages of 1848.

# SEVEN

## *Monarchy in England*

The English monarchy has never been absolute and no attempt to impose it as such on the governance of England has ever succeeded. There has always been some body of advisers standing in the way of would-be despots: the Anglo-Saxon witenagemot, the nobles, and ultimately parliament have all claimed the right to advise the king, and not only claimed it, but fought for it and forced it on monarchs who attempted to keep it from them. This did more than place kings in Parliament's power. It preserved them from the dangers of the Divine Right which encouraged monarchies to stagnate in their own inflexibility and atrophied their willingness to accept or institute change. English-style monarchy, on the other hand, raised royalty above damaging controversies and allowed it to become more pliable and better able to develop in tune with changing times and changing political concepts. Ultimately, with the introduction of constitutional monarchy in 1689, there was room for both the king and his erstwhile opponents in the system known as 'King-in-Parliament', which has since proved able to live with modern democracy. Absolutism and the Divine Right could never have done that. Even so, this does not mean that kings enjoyed complete freedom to act before constitutional monarchy was introduced.

One of their greatest frustrations concerned money. Problems with the payment of taxes were so serious that, at times, they hampered the ability of medieval kings to wage war or even to defend their realm. However, monarchs were not entirely the innocent victims of their parsimonious subjects. Royal demands for taxes could be exorbitant. In 1198, when King Richard I – Richard the Lionheart – needed money for the setting up of a new forest for royal hunting, the chronicler Roger of Hoveden described it as 'a kind of torment

116

. . . begun by the justices of the forest to the confusion of all men.'
After 1275, near the start of the reign of King Edward I, a new form
of tax – on personal goods and property – was levied on several
occasions to provide an ongoing supply of money for royal
purposes. Some of the poorest of the king's subjects were so hard
pressed by the tax that they had to sell their seed corn, and so risk
starvation, in order to pay it.[1]

Despite this, the reign of King Edward I was a milestone in the
relationship between monarch and Parliament, for the business of
legislation, as well as the raising of money for royal purposes, was
shared between them. By the mid-fourteenth century, the process of
'King-in-Parliament' had become normal in the conduct of
government affairs, whereas in countries where monarchy was more
absolute, such as France, the king alone could legislate, unrestrained
by any advisory or other restrictive body. Parliament, though, was
not always a comfortable partner to work with, as successive
English monarchs soon discovered. Its members could be very mean
when it came to granting funds and they were perfectly capable of
using money as a weapon to blackmail concessions out of a
recalcitrant king. Meanwhile, increasingly sophisticated methods of
tax evasion were preventing sufficient funds from reaching the royal
exchequer. Under-assessment of property and land became so
common that in the fourteenth century, the tax yield from this
source was only one-third of the real values. Two centuries later, in
1507, towards the end of King Henry VII's reign, a Book of Rates
was issued, mainly for the Port of London: however, by this time
under-assessment had been honed to such a fine art that the value of
goods for customs purposes was cited at less than 15 per cent of
what they were really worth.

There was, too, a prevailing sentiment that taxation should be
imposed only in cases of national emergency, which normally meant
war or threatened invasion. Even then it was difficult to prise money
out of taxpayers and some parliaments put all sorts of obstacles in
the way of the king. Between 1472 and 1475, for example, the
House of Commons allowed King Edward IV a grant of money to
pay for his war against France, but only if the tax collected were

kept in a secure place and special permission were obtained before the king could get his hands on it.[2]

By these various means, the royal exchequer was consistently kept short of funds. Some people even baulked at paying for defence, using the 'not in my back yard' argument that the lords whose lands were directly at risk – like the Marcher lords who were confronted by Welsh rebels – should pay the cost of defending their territory. There were deaf ears for the argument that if the Marcher lords failed to keep back the Welsh, then the whole of the West Country and possibly the whole of England could be in danger.

Problems over money plagued the kings of England for centuries. Yet, alongside this, there was a popular cry for the monarch 'to live of his own', that is to support himself and his court and dispense royal patronage from the profits he derived from the crown lands and the customs system.[3] In 1449 and 1450, a few years before the start of the Wars of the Roses between the rival Plantagenet houses of York and Lancaster, the House of Commons demanded that royal patronage, which encouraged recipients to leech off the system, should be considerably reduced and the crown lands placed under direct management. That way, the king could gain the maximum cash out of his lands and, presumably, stop demanding taxes from his subjects.

This was known as 'endowed' monarchy. Although he was virtually forced into it, the system suited the purposes of Edward IV, the Yorkist claimant to the crown of England who displaced the Lancastrian incumbent, Henry VI, in 1461. As a king who had won his crown in battle – never a secure way of gaining a throne – Edward IV saw that his best bet for survival was his own self-sufficiency and a restoration of royal authority: this had steadily declined as the crown became poorer and the inelegant spectacle presented by the Wars of the Roses, of a royal family at war over the throne, reduced the kudos that was its due.

Fortunately, Edward was personally well equipped to operate the endowed monarchy. He had a keen business acumen that enabled him to go into business and amass his own fortune. The king traded in wool and tin and made a handsome profit out of shipping them to markets in Europe. Further profit came from the import duties, tonnage and poundage, which Edward owned for life, and he built up the royal estates until he owned 20 per cent of all the land in England. King Edward IV was a new kind of king. Still a warrior, with many battle victories to his name, he was also an entrepreneur handling his own finances and making his own deals. It was an innovation, but unfortunately it could not last. The endowed monarchy never quite managed to achieve a balance between cash flow and the giving of patronage, which tended to drain the royal resources beyond what they could stand.

The experiment with endowed monarchy was a failure, but Parliament came out of it in a much better position than the king. Its role in more or less forcing endowed monarchy on the king indicated the enhanced status it enjoyed in the fourteenth century and after. This status had not been easily gained. Violence, bloodshed, civil war and the merciless bullying of two monarchs, King John and his son King Henry III, were all involved before the barons, Parliament's predecessors, got what they wanted: the right to 'advise' the monarch, for which read 'control'. The famous Magna Carta, which King John was forced to sign at Runnymede in 1215, was not a charter of popular liberties, as is often thought: it set out the rights and privileges of the barons, and when the perfidious John reneged on the agreement, the result was civil war.

John died in 1216, shortly after the barons invited Louis Capet, heir to the French throne, to come to England and displace him. However, the barons had it all to do again when John's son, Henry III, succeeded his father. King Henry, too, had to be brought up short and prevented from having his despotic way by a document similar to Magna Carta – the Provisions of Oxford of 1258. Like his father before him, Henry caved in and signed. Like his father, he reneged and once again, civil war ensued. King Henry was taken prisoner at the Battle of Lewes on 14 May 1264 and so fell into the hands of his own brother-in-law, Simon de Montfort, Earl of Leicester. The king was not only Simon's prisoner but his hostage and his puppet. Simon intimidated Henry into signing laws and orders and in 1265 he called together an assembly of representatives from the shires and boroughs. Simon's purpose was to buttress his own power, but the long-term effect was to create the House of Commons and the start of Parliament's rise to supremacy in the governance of England. Simon de Montfort died the following year, killed at the Battle of Evesham by a hit squad sent against him by King Henry's son, the future Edward I.

Edward, who succeeded to the throne on his father's death in 1272, was canny enough to learn from King Henry's mistakes and those of his grandfather, King John. Edward reaffirmed the provisions of Magna Carta and treated Parliament as the way forward to a situation in which the people of England could have a greater voice in government, while still preserving the position of the king. Even so, the course of English history ensured that the way there was a very rocky one. Intelligent, responsive kings like Edward I who could recognise and cater for a shift in the national power balance were not exactly thick on the ground. In 1327, Edward's son, Edward II, and in 1399 his great-great-grandson, Richard II, ruined themselves by once again turning to their own favourites instead of their nobles for advice. Both kings were made to pay dearly for their errors. Both were forced to abdicate. Both were afterwards murdered.

Both, of course, had been anointed kings – the same 'Lord's anointed' to which the biblical books of Samuel so often referred.[4] The fact that they had been unworthy, even dangerous, was not good enough for the two kings who replaced them. Both Edward III, who succeeded his father, Edward II, and Henry IV, who became king in place of his cousin, Richard II, experienced acute guilt when they assumed the crown. The cause was not just superstitious fear over ill-treating God's choice. In England, the office of king had always been separate from the man who happened to be wearing the crown: kingship possessed a lustre all its own, eliciting wonder and awe. Deposing or killing a monarch therefore meant more than the downfall of one man: it was an offence against hallowed tradition and tantamount to treason.

In purely practical terms, the accession of Edward III may have occurred before the throne was properly due to him, but it did at least give England a respectable monarch in place of a much-hated renegade. The case of Henry IV was quite different and the consequences much more serious. Henry was a usurper, with no right to the throne: when he broke into the succession, he lit the fuse that eventually led to the Wars of the Roses, the savage contest between the Houses of York and Lancaster. This thirty-year struggle decimated the royal family and almost wiped out the nobility. In 1454, when the last Parliament before the wars convened, fifty-three adult peers of the realm attended. Just over thirty years later, when the final victor, Henry Tudor – King Henry VII – called his first parliament, only eighteen of them came. The rest were young, fatherless boys.

Tragic though this was, this situation gave King Henry VII a unique opportunity to remake the English nobility in his own image. The newly made peers appointed during Henry's reign owed their position solely to him and, theoretically at least, this gave him a more powerful position in England than any previous king had enjoyed. Henry VII was not particularly lovable and his avarice and harsh justice were difficult to endure. All the same, he gave England what it most needed after three decades of ruinous civil war: peace abroad and law and order at home, flourishing trade, and a use of the royal prerogatives that showed the king was fully in charge and unlikely to be unseated by rivals. For a country that had suffered so much upheaval and bloodshed for so long, these were welcome blessings and not surprisingly, Parliament, once so vociferous, fell relatively quiet during Henry's reign.

Nevertheless, it had a very active future. A new and unusual task awaited parliament after King Henry VIII succeeded his father in 1509. Henry, aged eighteen, became king at a time when monarchs were acquiring a new and glorious aura. The age of the warrior-king was largely over. The era of the Renaissance king had arrived. The currency of kingship was now a multiplicity of talents and in this area Henry VIII was superbly equipped. He was a gifted musician and dancer. He could cross intellectual swords with the great minds of the day. He and his first wife, Catherine of Aragon, kept a court that became known across Europe for its splendour, its artistry and its elaborate entertainments.

Henry seemed to be the king who had everything, except for the most important thing of all: a male heir to succeed him. Henry's solution to this problem could hardly have been more drastic. In order to divorce Catherine of Aragon and marry her lady-in-waiting, Anne Boleyn, a younger woman who could give him the son he craved, Henry took advantage of the Protestant movement that was dividing Europe to remove England from the jurisdiction of the Pope. The extensive legislation required to make this fundamental change was the work of Parliament, which was given a greater role in state affairs than it had ever enjoyed before. The fact that the break with Rome was entirely for King Henry's convenience had no effect on the great opportunity it offered Parliament to do more than simply advise the king or rubber-stamp the laws he wanted. Parliament became a power and a voice in its own right. That voice was going to be heard loud and clear once the Tudor dynasty came to an end on the death of Henry VIII's daughter, Elizabeth I, in 1603, and the accession of the first Stuart, King James VI of Scotland and James I of England.

Elizabeth I was most probably the cleverest of the Tudors but she was also the monarch who faced the most serious dangers, both personally and as queen. On both counts, Elizabeth was considered by many royal courts in Europe as illegitimate: her father's divorce from Catherine of Aragon was not recognised by Roman Catholics, so his second marriage, to Elizabeth's mother, Anne Boleyn, was considered illegal. It followed that as an illegitimate, Elizabeth had no right to be queen of England. The 'real' English monarch was Mary, Queen of Scots, who was descended from the eldest daughter of King Henry VII.

Elizabeth's position could hardly have been more precarious. It became even more so in 1570, when Pope Pius V excommunicated her. In his bull entitled *Regnans in Excelsis*, Pius proclaimed that Elizabeth, 'the pretended queen of England, the servant of wickedness . . . [has] incurred the sentence of excommunication and [will] be cut off from the Body of Christ. And moreover, we do declare her to be deprived of her pretended title to the kingdom aforesaid.'

In itself, excommunication meant little in Protestant England, but its connotations were fearful. Elizabeth's Catholic subjects were now free of their duty of loyalty towards her, and she was vulnerable to attack by any Catholic power that wanted to unseat her. This was not just theoretical: there was a very real danger that Spain or France – both infinitely richer and more influential than England, and the greatest military powers in the world – fully intended to invade, get rid of Elizabeth and replace her with Mary, Queen of Scots. The plots that surrounded Mary and eventually led to her execution in 1587 were rather more insidious, but they carried no less danger for Elizabeth. Most of them were backed by Elizabeth's major rival, King Philip II of Spain.

This situation forced the Tudor queen to live dangerously and throw up the greatest smokescreen ever used by an English monarch to conceal the perilous truth. To this end, Elizabeth virtually invented a glorious public image that appealed directly to patriotic Englishness. 'We Princes,' the queen told Parliament, 'are set as it were upon stages in the sight and view of the world.'

The way in which Elizabeth set herself up on a stage displayed all the Tudor mastery of propaganda, image-fixing and the cult of personality. It was so effective that, even today, her reign is widely regarded as a period of high achievement in which the glory of England was indelibly impressed upon the world. The desperate gamble that lay behind it, and the weakness and poverty of late Tudor England, were brilliantly concealed.

Elizabeth's greatest need was to be visible and at a time when communications were slow and the pervasive modern media did not exist, the only feasible method was the royal 'progress'. Elizabeth's progresses resembled a travelling theatre, and every summer of the first twenty years of her reign saw her moving in splendid procession through the major towns and cities of England. The centrepiece was the queen herself, a dazzling figure near-submerged in the jewels, brocade and ornaments of her dress, more like a living icon than a human being.

Elizabeth's subjects were awed and thrilled by the splendour of their queen. No monarch before her made so many public appearances, yet retained and even magnified the royal mystique. Her image – at once glamorous and aloof – was backed by poets, playwrights, painters, the creators of water pageants and masques at court, pamphleteers and ballad makers. All of them conspired to intensify the picture of Elizabeth as 'Gloriana' or 'The Faerie Queene' of Edmund Spenser's fantasy, touching all around her with her magic.

Behind the web of mystery that surrounded her, Elizabeth was playing a shrewd, though dangerous, diplomatic game, promising France and Spain the alliance with England that both wanted, but without ever reaching the point where the arrangement could be finalised. Similarly, Elizabeth secretly encouraged the impudent Sea Dogs – Francis Drake, John Hawkins, Martin Frobisher – to raid the jealously guarded Spanish colonies in America while making sure that her involvement could never be proved. Elizabeth kept suitors for her hand in suspense, never saying 'Yes', never saying 'No', but teasing them with sufficient hope to keep them interested. One of Elizabeth's most persistent suitors, François, Duc d'Alençon, wooed her for almost twenty years; the poor man was still hoping to marry her when she was in her forties. Elizabeth, of course, never married. In these various ways, the first thirty years of Elizabeth's reign were one great big gamble, a gamble that England and its queen would survive to finally reach a modicum of security in a hostile Europe. That stage was not reached until 1588, when tiny pipsqueak England, as the country was widely regarded, laid low the mighty Armada, the pride of Spain.

Compared to Elizabeth's knife-edge existence, her Stuart successor in 1603, James VI of Scotland, son of Mary Queen of Scots, came to the throne in a mood of supreme self-confidence as an experienced monarch who, he said, needed no lessons from the English Parliament. James could not have been more wrong. He had a great deal to learn – about England, the English, their Parliament and above all, his position and his powers as king. King James made his ideas on the subject uncomfortably clear in a speech he made to Parliament in 1610.

The state of monarchy is the supremest thing upon earth; for kings are not only God's lieutenants upon earth . . . but even by God himself are called gods. . . . Kings are justly called gods, for that they exercise a manner or resemblance of divine power upon earth . . . God hath power to create or destroy make or unmake at His pleasure, to give life or send death, to judge all and to be judged nor accountable to none. . . . And the like power have kings: they make and unmake their subjects, they have power of raising and casting down, of life and of death, judges over all their subjects and in all causes and yet accountable to none but God only. . . . That as to dispute what God may do is blasphemy . . . so is it sedition in subjects to dispute what a king may do in the height of his power.

This was bad news for Parliament, which had no intention of giving up one jot of the hard-won rights they had acquired during centuries of struggle. However, the guardians of those rights were no longer the aristocracy. By the early seventeenth century, the balance of power within Parliament had shifted from the House of Lords to the House of Commons, and the latter contained an added ingredient that made James's sentiments not only unwelcome but dangerous. The Puritans, so called because of their ascetic religious views, were not a large element in Parliament or in the country, but they were vociferous, single-minded and highly critical of what they saw as the 'popery', materialism, greed and tyranny in the Church of England.

There were, perhaps, up to 350 Puritan ministers and 100,000 laymen in England at the turn of the seventeenth century,[5] and their aim was to recreate the Kingdom of Heaven on Earth, making God's law as laid down in the Bible the one and only form of guidance. In the ideal Puritan world there were no hierarchies, no bishops and no kings, since any form of control by one man or group over another was tyranny. This was revolutionary thinking. Puritan ideas of personal freedom and freedom of conscience were barely permissible in the seventeenth century and where they existed they were often treated – and punished – as heresy.

Thomas Cartwright, Professor of Divinity at Cambridge University, was the major proponent of the Puritan creed during the reign of Elizabeth I. Cartwright's argument against the paramountcy of kings went like this:

> . . . they must remember to subject themselves unto the church, to submit their sceptres, to throw down their crowns, before the church. . . . Whatsoever magnificence, or excellency, or pomp, is either in them, or in their estates and commonwealths, which doth not agree with the simplicity . . . of the church, that they will be content to lay down.

This was sedition. The right of kings to rule had never before been challenged in such terms. Inevitably, Cartwright was made to suffer for his views. He was stripped of his professorship and thrown out of Cambridge in 1571. He took shelter abroad, in Switzerland, where the Calvinists, who were of like ascetic mind, welcomed him. He tried to return several times but England was too unsafe for him. In fact, all Puritans were in danger of punishment after the Elizabethan Act against Puritans became law in 1593. Cartwright died in 1603,[6] the year of King James's accession to his English throne.

James had been king for barely a month before thirteen eminent Puritan divines presented him with the Millenary Petition asking for reforms in the Church of England and in the position and function of the bishops. James refused to make any changes: he asserted that he would have only 'one doctrine, and one discipline, one religion in substance and in ceremony'. In his famous phrase: 'No bishop, no king!' James also reiterated his belief that monarchy and episcopacy were indissolubly bound together.[7]

Far from accommodating the Puritan demands, James went the opposite way and relaxed the laws against their principal *bêtes-noires*, the Roman Catholics. So many closet Catholics came out of hiding that the king became frightened. He clamped down again. One of the results was the famous Gunpowder Plot of 1605, which was brewed by discontented Catholics furious at the chance of freedom James had first offered, then snatched away.

James's reign had hardly started on an auspicious note and as the years passed the situation did not improve. James's belief in the Divine Right of Kings was never shaken and he presented Parliament with an ongoing series of grievances: reliance on favourites as ministers and advisers, raising taxes, taking personal charge of foreign policy and committing the ultimate offence, ruling without Parliament. Old age and senility rescued King James from the worst consequences of his actions, and in 1624 he granted Parliament everything its members wanted, including the right to have a say in foreign policy. The problem was not yet over, though. James's successor, his son King Charles I, was another adherent of the Divine Right of Kings and had learned nothing from his father's experience. Consequently, the early years of Charles's reign saw a repeat performance of his father's – the favourites, the personal taxation, rule without Parliament – but there was one crucial difference. James I had exasperated Parliament and they had fought him fiercely, but they always remained loyal to him as king. By the time Charles I came to the throne, the mood had changed. The Puritans had become much more influential in the House of Commons and, disliking kings as they did, they were less prepared to put up with Charles's despotic behaviour.

This time, though, there was no last minute climb-down on the part of the king, but a hardening of attitudes and enmities which could have only one, disastrous, outcome: civil war. The internecine conflict that lasted from 1642 to the capture of King Charles late in 1648 was a struggle for dominance between absolute, exclusive royal power, as embodied by the king, and the representative power of Parliament. The latter prevailed and, in January 1649, put Charles on trial at Westminster Hall, London. The king, unable to see beyond his Divine Right, refused to recognise the legality of the court.

At the trial, which opened on 20 January 1649, Charles was impeached 'as a Tyrant, Traitor, Murderer, and a public and implacable Enemy to the Commonwealth of England'. He was accused of devising 'a wicked design to erect and uphold in himself an unlimited and tyrannical power to rule according to his Will, and to overthrow the Rights and Liberties of the People'. In addition, he had 'traitorously and maliciously levied war against the present Parliament and the people therein represented [with the sole objective of] upholding of a personal interest of Will and Power and pretended prerogative to himself and his family against the public interest, common right, liberty, justice and peace of the people of this nation'.

Charles refused to answer the charges or to defend himself. Instead, he told the court:

> I would know by what power I am called hither . . . I would know by what authority, I mean lawful. . . . Remember, I am your King, your lawful King, and what sins you bring upon your heads, and the judgment of God upon this land. Think well upon it, I say, think well upon it, before you go further from one sin to a greater. . . . I have a trust committed to me by God, by old and lawful descent, I will not betray it, to answer a new unlawful authority . . . I do stand more for the liberty of my people, than any here that come to be my pretended judges. . . . Let me see a legal authority warranted by the Word of God, the Scriptures, or warranted by the constitutions of the Kingdom, and I will answer.
>
> It is not a slight thing you are about. I am sworn to keep the peace, by that duty I owe to God and my country; and I will do it to the last breath of my body . . . a King cannot be tried by any superior jurisdiction on earth . . .

All that remained now was to find the king guilty and pass sentence. The sentence, inevitably, was death 'by severing of his head from his body'. A total of 135 judges had been summoned to Westminster Hall to try the king; however, all but 68 of them stayed away, unwilling at the last moment to be involved in judging a monarch. Nine of the 68 refused to sign the royal death warrant, leaving only 59 judges, including Oliver Cromwell, who were willing to attach their signatures.

The date of King Charles's execution was set for 30 January 1649, and a large scaffold was specially built outside the Banqueting Hall in Whitehall. It was bitterly cold and the king asked for two shirts to keep him warm because, he said: 'The season is so sharp as probably may make me shake, which some observers may imagine proceeds from fear. I would have no such imputation.'

There was a delay in the execution when the headsman detailed for the task refused to perform it. Another executioner and assistant were found, but they insisted on wearing masks so that no one would know their identities. When Charles was brought to the scaffold, a large crowd was there to watch. When he spoke to them, it was clear that nothing that had happened had changed his mind.

'I must tell you,' he said, 'that the liberty and freedom [of the people] consists in having of Government, those laws by which their life and their goods may be most their own. It is not for having share in Government, that is nothing pertaining to them. A subject and a sovereign are clean different things.'

The executioner cut off Charles's head with a single blow. As he did so, wrote one eyewitness, 'there was such a groan by the thousands then present, as I never heard before and desire I may never hear again'. The magic of monarchy still had such a hold, even on an occasion like this, that many spectators came forward to dip their handkerchiefs in Charles's blood, believing that it would heal wounds and cure illnesses.

The same day, an Act was hastily passed by Parliament forbidding the proclamation of a new monarch, a device to prevent Charles's son, the future King Charles II, from claiming the throne. Eight days later, the English monarchy was abolished and for the first and only time in its history, England became a republic.

It was not that easy to consign monarchy to the past. Despite their seizure of power in England, the Puritans never succeeded in winning over large numbers of adherents to their strict concept of Christianity. Nor did they win sanction for their view of kings as tyrants. What the Puritans soon discovered was that royalty had a hold on the public imagination no Act of Parliament or theological argument could shift. Oliver Cromwell, proclaimed Lord Protector in 1653, had none of the magic of a monarch, despite his extensive powers. The attempt by some Members of Parliament to add to

Cromwell's lustre by offering him the crown in 1657 was not feasible, since getting rid of one monarch and replacing him with another made nonsense of all the Puritan Parliament had fought for. It was nevertheless ironic that Oliver Cromwell was more of an absolute ruler than any king of England had ever managed to be. When he died in 1658, it became clear that the continuance of the English republic depended on him, and only him. Once he was gone and his incompetent son, Richard, succeeded him, anarchy soon ensued.

At this juncture, the only possible solution was to recall the king – the real king, Charles – from exile. Only a king, endowed with the traditional mystique, would be able to restore England to some sort of order. Colonel George Monck, the architect of the king's return in 1660, had made a very popular choice, as was evident when Charles II entered London on 29 May, his thirtieth birthday, and the city went wild with joy. John Evelyn, the diarist, described the scene:

> The triumph of above 20,000 horse and foot brandishing their swords and shouting with inexpressible joy: The ways were strewed with flowers, the bells ringing, the streets hung with tapestry, fountains ran with wine: the Mayor, Aldermen and all the companies in their liveries, chains of gold and banners: Lord and nobles clad in cloth of silver and gold and velvet: the windows and balconies well set with ladies: trumpets, music and myriads of people flocking . . . so they were seven hours in passing the City [of London] even from two in the afternoon till nine at night.

That night, there were fireworks and illuminations over the River Thames. Boats and barges moored on the river were crammed with spectators, so many, Evelyn wrote, that 'you could have walked across [the river]'.

However, Charles II returned from his twelve-year exile in Europe with more than personal popularity to help him in his greatest quest – 'never to go on [his] travels again.' As events soon proved, King Charles would do virtually anything to retain his throne. For example, in 1670 and again in 1678, Charles accepted secret payments from King Louis XIV of France for a purpose that was, in fact, illegal: the king wanted to be free of Parliament and the need to ask that body for money. By 1681, Charles at last became self-sufficient. He dissolved Parliament and ruled without it until his death in 1685.

Some Members of Parliament suspected that there were secret clauses in the treaties with France, but they did not attempt to pin the king down over them. Once there would have been uproar as the king failed to call a Parliament for years on end, but fears of another civil war and residual remorse over the execution of his father allowed Charles II to get away with it.

His French pay packet was not the only thing Charles kept secret from Parliament. He, too, possessed the Stuart devotion to the Divine Right of Kings and although he was far too canny to express it openly, it was obvious in some of his actions.

The greatest issue of Charles II's reign concerned his brother and heir presumptive, James, Duke of York. James became controversial in 1671, when he became a Roman Catholic. It was the worst possible timing. Catholics were anathema in strongly Protestant England, and in 1673 parliament passed the Test Act which required anyone taking public office to take communion according to the Church of England. This effectively barred Catholics and all other non-Anglicans from positions of importance. James refused to take the Anglican sacrament and resigned his post as Lord Admiral. However, his eventual position, as king of England, was no ordinary public office. To increase alarm at the prospect of his succession, James made it clear that as monarch, he intended to restore Catholicism in England and return the country to the jurisdiction of the Pope.

This set off a vicious struggle, the Exclusion Crisis, aimed at removing James from the succession to the throne. It raged for two years until 1681, and during those two years, every move made by James's enemies, the Whigs, was blocked by King Charles who used his royal prerogative to close down the debate. Finally, Charles gave a dramatic demonstration of who was master when he summoned a Parliament at Oxford in March 1681. The Whig lords, confident of victory, arrived at Oxford only to find the king seated on his throne in full regalia, the epitome of majesty. It was a splendid, but also a daunting sight and a show of royal grandeur the Whigs could not ignore.

James remained heir to his brother's throne even though, privately, Charles was convinced that as king, he would ruin himself within three years. Charles's arithmetic was exactly right. As King James II after 1685, James used his royal prerogative to restore Catholicism in England, just as he had promised. Anglicans seethed as Catholics were given high and important posts. There was uproar at Oxford and Cambridge where the universities were obliged to admit Catholic students. Parliament was enraged in 1687 when James issued a Declaration of Indulgence suspending all penal laws and also claimed the right to dispose of any law that did not meet with his approval.

However, James's safeguard was the same as his late brother's: no one wanted another civil war and no one had the heart to kill another king. The only comfort in this situation lay with Mary and Anne, King James's two Protestant daughters by his first marriage. Both of them were married to Protestant princes, Mary to William of Orange and Anne to Prince George of Denmark. One day, either or both of these women would become reigning queens, backed by the appropriate consorts, and the Catholic menace would be gone for ever.

Then, suddenly, this neat plan for the Protestant future of the Stuart dynasty went awry. On 10 June 1688, to the surprise of everyone, including his parents, a son, James Edward Stuart, was born to the king's second, Catholic, wife, Mary of Modena. He was their first child in fifteen years of marriage. Now, an endless line of Catholic monarchs stretched far into the future. There was only one solution: James, his Catholic wife and his Catholic son had to go. In a desperate throw that skirted the edge of treason, seven prominent men, including a former bishop of London, secretly contacted William of Orange and asked him to rescue England from Catholic disaster. William, known as the 'Protestant Saviour' of Europe, arrived from Holland on 5 November 1688.

This threat from his own son-in-law terrified King James. He became afraid that he was going to share his father's fate, and on 11 December 1688, he attempted to slip away to France, disguised as a woman. A group of fishermen recognised him and brought him back, but he was given every encouragement to try again and finally reached France on Christmas Day. Mary of Modena and their infant son soon followed him into exile.

The 'Glorious Revolution', as it was called, had been carried through without war or bloodshed, but the successful, if abrupt, alteration in the royal succession had raised its problems. A convention of Members of Parliament met in February 1689 to decide the succession to the throne, but at once came up against an immovable obstacle: William of Orange had no intention of bailing out the English and then retiring into second place while his wife, Mary, became reigning queen. As a grandson of King Charles I, and therefore Mary's first cousin, William had some claim to the English throne himself. That, though, was less important than William's position *vis-à-vis* his great enemy, the Catholic King Louis XIV of France. William's great crusade in life was to overcome the powerful and aggressive Louis, who was threatening the very existence of tiny Holland. To accomplish this task, William believed, he had to have a status equal to his rival's. In this context, the invitation to save England for the Protestant faith had come as a godsend. It gave William the chance to make the English an offer they could not refuse: either they made him king or he would return to Holland with his army and let them stew.

Faced with King William or no William, the convention had to concede. They offered the crown jointly to William and Mary, who, as King William III and Queen Mary II, became the only married couple ever to ascend the throne of England. All the same, the convention had the last word. They had to protect themselves, their liberties and England.

England, they knew, was going to become involved in William's war against King Louis, and that meant taxes, manpower and resources, all of them being consumed at the behest of a foreigner. And if there was anything the English had always hated with a passion, it was foreign rule, foreign wars and being made to dance to a foreign tune. Besides this, William and Mary were Stuarts and there was no guarantee that, once full royal powers were theirs, they would shrink from exercising the Divine Right that was virtually a family tradition.

The Bill of Rights, the safeguard introduced in 1689 to curb the powers of the crown, was the great turning point in the history of the English monarchy, marking the moment when Parliament finally prevailed over unrestricted royal power. 'Constitutional monarchy', the term coined to cover this radical shift of political emphasis, was something of a euphemism. This new and unique form of monarchy was more of an emasculation, depriving the monarch of some of his most important powers and placing him under the tutelage of Parliament.

The monarch lost age-old rights and prerogatives: the right to make war, the right to raise and maintain a standing army, the right to raise taxes, the ability to use the royal prerogatives to obstruct legislation, and the power, claimed by the earlier Stuarts, to tell the House of Commons what they might and might not discuss. History crowded in on an epoch-making moment during the coronation of the new king and queen, which took place at Westminster Abbey on 11 April 1689. For the first time, the coronation oath included a royal promise to obey the laws of Parliament, including the Bill of Rights. In England, the days of arbitrary royal rule were over. Here, at least, the Divine Right of Kings was dead.

# EIGHT

## *Constitutional Monarchy*

During the nineteenth and into the twentieth century, when European thrones were largely monopolised by autocrats, the British monarchy was regarded, at best, as a paltry shadow of the world's oldest and most prestigious form of government. From this viewpoint, British monarchs were tantamount to puppets. They bore magnificent titles: they were commanders of the armed forces, supreme governors of the Church of England, emperors of India and sovereigns over the world-wide British Empire, yet they had no power to act or make their own decisions in any of these capacities. They had been stripped of the royal prerogatives, which were now exercised by Parliament. They depended on Parliament for their pay. In politics, British monarchs were upstaged by prime ministers and their cabinets. At the same time, Parliament exercised a will of its own which, by law, could supervene that of the king.

This was, of course, the highly prejudiced view of monarchs weaned on a diet of absolute power, God-given rights and deference that was little different from worship. Nevertheless, the limitations imposed on kings by constitutional monarchy were real enough. King Edward VII was given a sharp lesson in where the parameters lay after he came to the English throne in 1901. Edward was anxious to be an active monarch, concerning himself with government business and the workings of Parliament. No chance. The king was politely, but firmly, told to keep his hands off concerns that were beyond his purview. Politically, the involvement he planned would be seen as undue interference with the rights of the real rulers of Britain – the Members of Parliament and the voters who elected them.

135

Emperors, kings and even dukes who ruled by Divine Right and imposed their will upon their realms were astounded at the way the king of England could be told what he could and could not do by his own subjects. To them, British constitutional monarchy was no more than a charade. What they did not realise was that this seemingly watered-down version of monarchy did not demean, but actually preserved the monarch: it raised him above embarrassing disputes, and separated him from the most common sources of friction – political rivalries, faction fighting, taxation, war and the sufferings and deprivations caused by war.

Unlike the king of England, autocrats were directly in the line of fire on all these counts, for they were personally linked to the fate of their realms. As a result, a fearful lesson was brought home to three absolute monarchies in Europe after the First World War ended in 1918: Kaiser Wilhelm II of Germany, the Austrian Hapsburg Emperor Karl I and Tsar Nicholas II of Russia were all dethroned by popular uprisings. Emperor Karl fell victim to the urge for independence among the four nations – Austria, Hungary, Czechoslovakia, Yugoslavia – that made up his empire. The kaiser and the tsar failed to read the warning signals of popular unrest and the activities of radicals and communists who sought to exploit it. Their involvement in the conduct of the war exposed them to personal blame for the sufferings of their subjects, the kaiser through his militaristic policies, the tsar by his assumption of military command, which he had neither the training nor the talent to handle. Together with a fourth loser in the war, the Ottoman Turkish sultan, Abdul Mejid II, Kaiser Wilhelm and the Austrian emperor were removed from power and forced into exile. Tsar Nicholas was murdered. Subsequently, Germany, Austria, Russia and Turkey became republics.

Meanwhile, in Britain, the monarchy not only survived intact but did so with increased prestige. This did not mean that republican and other agitators and potential revolutionaries were dormant. In 1921, there was a wave of hissing when the king's name was mentioned at a Communist rally in London. In 1922, Sir Arthur Bigge, Lord Stamfordham, King George V's private secretary, wrote to Prime Minister Andrew Bonar Law:

The King is daily growing more anxious about the question of unemployment during the coming winter. . . . The people grow discontented and agitators seize their opportunities; marches are organised; the police interfere; resistance ensues; troops are called out and riot begets revolt and possibly revolution.[1]

What neither Stamfordham nor King George seemed to realise was that the monarch had already taken out personal insurance against downfall: he had earned personal popularity and commended himself to his suffering subjects by identifying himself and the royal family with Britain at war. For example, the king imposed a spartan regime on the royal household. Luxury foods like lamb or the succulent *poussin* were banned: their place was taken by ordinary fowl and mutton. The royal family had to reuse their table napkins instead of receiving a new one with every meal. Royal dinners were very plain. Mrs John Fortescue, wife of the royal librarian, recorded one menu: 'Mulligatawny soup,' she wrote, 'turbot, shrimp sauce; vegetable cutlets, green peas, new potatoes, asparagus, cold baked custard in china cups . . .' Although the royal family were not exactly starving themselves, it was a great contrast to the life of plenty and luxury they had enjoyed before the war.[2]

The king himself went into uniform for the duration and tirelessly toured hospitals, munitions factories and shipyards: he made 450 visits to the troops, and despite having to steel himself against seasickness, he dutifully inspected scores of Royal Navy vessels riding at anchor. George V's queen, Mary, concerned herself with soldiers' charities. His daughter, the Princess Royal, worked as a nurse. His heir, Edward, Prince of Wales, the future King Edward VIII, defied official objections to the risks he was taking, and saw for himself the action in the trenches in France: in 1915, at Béthune, the prince was within a few hundred yards of the enemy lines and came under shellfire. In addition, there were snipers nearby.[3] King George's second son, Albert, the future George VI, served in the naval Battle of Jutland in 1916 before being invalided out with a stomach ulcer.

After the war, despite the king's fears, republican agitation proved ephemeral and among the royal houses of Europe there was no one left to point a scornful finger at the British royals and call them puppets. Apart from the obvious changes introduced into the role of kings, constitutional monarchy had boosted a crucial factor which, to their appalling cost, absolutists and autocrats had ignored: the ability to evolve.

Because of this process, the constitutional position of King Edward VII or King George V in the early twentieth century was radically different from that of the joint Stuart monarchs, William and Mary, who were the first to come under Parliament's control. At that time, constitutional monarchy was a unique idea that contradicted everything that had ever been believed about the role and rights of kings. Initially, though, it was able to put down roots in England because of a mutually agreeable trade-off between King William and Parliament. William needed the resources of Britain in his struggle to prevent Louis XIV of France from overrunning his Dutch homeland. However, these resources were available to William only by the consent of Parliament, and Parliament was accessible to him only if he accepted the conditions of constitutional monarchy. Both Parliament and king got what they wanted – the defeat of the Catholic King James for the one, and for the other, the rescue of Holland from the clutches of the French. However, for Parliament, an extra task lay ahead: finalising constitutional monarchy to confirm its own ascendancy.

This was largely achieved in 1701 when Parliament restructured the monarchy once again. William and Mary had no surviving children and after Mary's death from smallpox in 1694, her younger sister Anne postponed her own accession to allow William to retain the throne until his death. In 1700, however, the last of Anne's surviving children died: that left only Catholic Stuarts as the next heirs to the Crown. The Protestant Parliament would have none of that. They sought out the nearest Protestant heir, the elderly Sophia, electress of Hanover, who was, technically, only fifty-second in line to the throne. Nevertheless, Sophia was descended from King James I, the first Stuart monarch, through his daughter Elizabeth, and that made her eligible to jump the queue ahead of all those other, Catholic, claimants.

The deal was concluded in the Act of Settlement of 1701, which settled the throne on Sophia and her descendants after Anne's death. Arrangements for the Protestant succession were not the only feature of the Act. Its other provisions placed further restrictions on the monarch. Future sovereigns had to be members of the Anglican Church of England. English monarchs, present and future, were also to lose the power to dismiss judges, unless Parliament specifically requested it. If Parliament impeached a government minister, the monarch would no longer be able to come to the rescue and grant a pardon.

When William died in 1702 after a fall from his horse and Queen Anne succeeded him, she therefore acquired a throne well and truly hedged about with limitations, with crucially reduced room for royal manoeuvre. Anne has often been depicted as fat, foolish and firmly under the thumb of her favourite, Sarah Churchill, Duchess of Marlborough. Anne, however, was not as supine as historians have long made out. First of all, she understood very well the one power that Parliament could never match: the almost supernatural aura that had long attached itself to English monarchs. Anne exploited this by continuing the ancient ritual of 'touching for the King's evil': the 'evil' in question was scrofula, probably a form of tuberculosis, and the belief that the royal touch could cure it went back to medieval times. The renowned Dr Samuel Johnson, for one, remembered being touched by the lady who wore a black hood and diamonds: the queen's touch failed to cure him, but Johnson never forgot her air of majesty.[4]

Although she was a Stuart, from a glamorous, dynamic dynasty that had the Divine Right of Kings in its genes, Anne knew she could never use it in earnest. Even so, she insisted on making her own decisions when it came to choosing candidates for church appointments. Likewise, when it came to selecting ministers, ambassadors or officials, Anne's personal choices frequently prevailed. In 1708, in a move that has never happened since, Anne used her power of veto and declined to give the Royal Assent to a parliamentary bill: this one put the Scots militia on the same footing as the militia in England. The royal veto killed the bill. The power game worked both ways, though, and in the same year parliamentary muscle asserted itself when the queen was obliged to concede victory to the Whigs. They had won a majority in the House of Commons and, much against her will, Anne was obliged to admit them to her cabinet.

Gradually, Parliament was building on its own creation, constitutional monarchy, to strengthen its hold over the monarch. The queen, for instance, normally presided over cabinet meetings and sometimes attended debates in the House of Lords. However, Anne's political abilities were minimal and she tended to lapse into figurehead mode while minds that were more acutely tuned to politics dominated cabinet business. Parliament's dominance over the sovereign was furthered by a special parliamentary grant for the upkeep of the royal household: the Civil List. This was the grant that made the sovereign a pensioner of the state[5] and also underlined the rise of the aristocracy to unprecedented heights of wealth, status and power.

As a result, they were massively self-confident, a feeling crystallised by their often stupendous wealth. The Duke of Newcastle owned thousands of acres in thirteen English counties, together with an income from rents of up to £40,000 a year. The dukes of Bedford were rich enough to own three or four palaces and the dukes of Buccleuch could boast eight country houses and two London mansions when building just one in a suitably splendid manner ran well into six figures. As time went on, the cult of the country house heaped luxury upon luxury until palaces and mansions were crammed with every possible refinement, from the carvings on gilt chandeliers to the filigree on door locks, the embossed figurework on silver to the rococo twirls and marquetry on furniture.

The magnificence in which the English aristocracy lived and the money they spent so freely reflected privileges that had been far beyond the reach of their ancestors. Now, the aristocracy looked on themselves as king makers and control of their royal creation was sanctioned by law and expressed in a parliament filled from their ranks. In the circumstances of 1701 and the Act of Settlement, it was just as well that Parliament was fully equipped with pride of achievement, a sense of its own dominance and a resolve never again to be outclassed by kings. Parliament was going to need all its new-found muscle when, in 1714, it was faced with the new, Hanoverian, dynasty that not only had its own prior realm, the Electorate, but ruled it by Divine Right, as autocrats.

Both Queen Anne and the Electress Sophia of Hanover died in 1714, and the new monarch who arrived in Britain on 18 September that year was Sophia's son, King George I.[6] George was, of course, accustomed to the freedom given him by absolute monarchy in Hanover, where his word was law and his presence was hallowed. His portrait, which was placed on his throne at the Herrenhausen Palace, served to represent him while he was away in England and became an object of veneration. King George was unused to criticism or resistance and ruled Hanover in easygoing, paternalistic fashion. It therefore came as quite a shock to encounter the feisty English Parliament which had already appropriated royal powers long before the Hanoverians arrived. Just as foreign to the Hanoverian scheme of things was the English populace, which was free to voice its own opinions and was prone to express its discontent by vociferous protest and even revolt.

For absolute rulers to fit into a new role as constitutional monarchs was therefore the ultimate exercise of square pegs in round holes. It was a considerable challenge and a severe test for the institution, which was still only a quarter of a century old when George I came to the throne. However, Parliament had not come this far merely to be trounced by a potential despot, and although they struggled against it at first, the Hanoverians made no serious attempt to upend the unfamiliar style of monarchy they found in Britain. Nor did the British show any real desire to pack them off back to Hanover: they failed to respond to the chance they were offered in the Jacobite rebellions of 1715 and 1745 which sought to restore the Stuarts to the throne. In this case, the Stuarts, the devils they knew, were not preferable when the Stuart century had meant so much religious and political strife, and so little personal freedom.

Britain and its foreign monarchs therefore made an 'odd couple' and settling down to live together was an awkward process. The first two Georges were personally unpopular, mainly due to their open dislike of Britain and the British and the way in which they wriggled hard against the restraints imposed on them. Legislation passed in the reigns of William III and Queen Anne restricted them at almost every turn. They were forbidden to grant peerages, public office or lands to foreigners, even to those who were naturalised British. Though they retained the right to create new ministerial posts, no one appointed to these posts could voice the royal opinions in the House of Commons. The king could still appoint judges, but since he was banned from dismissing them, he had no control over judicial decisions.

At every turn, the fact was emphasised that but for Parliament, the Hanoverians would never have inherited the English throne. As dependents as well as pensioners of Parliament, it was difficult for them to acquire the allure the Stuarts or the Tudors had possessed in such great measure. Given the frustrations involved in being kings in England, it was hardly surprising that the first two Georges frequently escaped to Hanover, where the far less fractious atmosphere was balm to their autocratic souls.[7]

King George I was absent in Hanover on seven occasions during his thirteen-year reign. His absences lasted, on average, for six months, which meant that he spent around a quarter of his reign away from his kingdom. When he died in 1727, he was once more on his way to his Electorate.

During his reign of thirty-three years, George II went to Hanover eleven times, also for an average six months for each visit. He made no secret of his dislike of Britain, the British, their Parliament, their government and everything to do with all of them. 'I wish with all my heart that the devil take your [Prime] Minister,' he once exploded in a rage, 'and the devil take the Parliament, and the devil take the whole island, provided I can get out of it and go to Hanover.'

Even in an emergency it was difficult to tempt the king back to England. George II was in his Electorate in 1755, when the Seven Years' War with France was imminent, and considerable pressure had to be exerted on him to make him return to Britain. King George did not give in without a struggle. 'There are kings enough in England,' he said, referring to Members of Parliament. 'I am nothing there. I am old' – he was seventy-three years of age – 'and want rest and should only go to be plagued and teased there about that damned House of Commons.'[8]

George II had not forgotten a lesson in the limitations of constitutional monarchy which he received shortly after he became king. His first son, Prince Frederick, now twenty-one, arrived in England in 1728 to take up his new position as heir to the throne. King George, however, hated Frederick and once said of him: 'He is a monster and the greatest villain ever born . . . the greatest ass and the greatest liar . . . and the greatest beast in the whole world and I heartily wish he was out of it!' Frederick obliged, dying in 1751, nine years before his father. For as long as it lasted, though, the confrontation of king and prince was savage. For example, King George did his best to prevent Frederick receiving the title Prince of Wales which had been borne by heirs to the throne of England for more than four centuries. He became enraged when told by his ministers that Frederick had every right to the title and that it could not be denied him. Forced to give in, the king was openly resentful when he had to allow Frederick to be proclaimed Prince of Wales in January 1729. As a Parthian shot, King George refused to allow Frederick to carry out any official functions.

This shaming experience, in which Frederick's rights were shown to be superior to his father's wishes, hit the royal ego very hard and strengthened George II's resolve to be an active monarch, formulating his own policy and making his own decisions. Although this plan appeared despotic, it did not contravene the rules of constitutional monarchy as they existed in the reigns of the first two Georges.

However much he baulked at the restraints, King George was not entirely devoid of personal power and influence. Like his father, he cited the traditional role of the king as military commander to claim royal control of the army. He reinforced his claim when he became the last king of England to take personal command of his forces in the field, at the Battle of Dettingen in 1743. Foreign affairs was another area in which the kings claimed an active role, and here their claim had some validity. George I and George II had a real understanding of the foreign scene. They were more familiar than their ministers with political developments in Germany, which was an increasingly important focus of European politics in the eighteenth century.

In England, a major source of royal power was financial. Although the Civil List was a parliamentary allowance, the king received the money for life and had a large measure of control over how it was used. He was able, for example, to award pensions to his favourites. He could use the money to buy the votes of politicians in Parliament, so exerting an influence over elections. He could buy a stake, as it were, in the loyalties of his chief ministers and secretaries of state since they depended on monies from the Civil List as part of their income. In a sense, this made them servants of the king first, and ministers afterwards.

Like Queen Anne and King George I, George II had the right to choose his ministers and this enabled him to keep Sir Robert Walpole in power long after Walpole had lost the confidence of both Parliament and the people. Eventually, in 1742, Walpole succumbed to a series of defeats in the House of Commons and even the king had to realise it was the end and reluctantly accepted his minister's resignation.[9]

The five years before he was forced to leave office – after two decades as chief minister – had been particularly difficult for Walpole. In 1737, with the death of George II's queen, Caroline, he had lost his best political ally. George II was not an easy man to deal with. Bad-tempered, immensely conceited and arrogantly intent on making up his own mind, the king had to be cajoled into going along with Walpole's political line. Fortunately, Queen Caroline, an extremely clever woman of great charm, whose plump full breasts held her husband virtually in thrall, was an expert at persuading him to her way of thinking. What King George never realised was that Caroline's way of thinking was also Walpole's, for the two of them discussed the latest political questions in private before the minister arrived at the palace for his meeting with the king.

The queen was there, doing her embroidery. She appeared for all the world like the 'little woman' sitting in the background, where she belonged, while the men arranged the affairs of the world. As the discussions progressed, the queen and Walpole used a series of secret hand signals as comments on the way the talks were going. Walpole would play with his hat. Or he took snuff or pulled his handkerchief from his pocket. Caroline signalled back by raising her fan or threading a needle. The king never noticed the charade and ended his audience with Walpole convinced that the policies on which they had agreed were all his own idea.[10]

Queen Caroline was crucial to the smooth working of this arrangement and when she died in 1738, Walpole considered it 'the greatest blow he had ever received'. Carrying on without her seemed impossible and Walpole seriously considered resigning. Although he continued in office out of loyalty to the dead queen and to King George, he found it increasingly difficult to guide the monarch as easily as before. In 1739, for example, King George declared war on Spain against Walpole's advice.

Walpole, who fell from power three years later, suffered a similar fate to the royal favourite who, historically, had been a familiar figure in the courts of Queen Elizabeth I or her Stuart successors. The favourite relied for power on the goodwill and support of a single patron but once that patron was gone or the goodwill was withdrawn, downfall was inevitable. By Walpole's time, however, advancement along these lines was giving way to a different strategy. Henry Pelham, a keen supporter of Walpole, succeeded him as chief minister in 1743. Pelham once outlined the strategy which became possible under constitutional monarchy at a time when the powers of the king and the powers of Parliament were more or less in balance. Pelham believed that if he were unable to gain the support of Parliament, then the backing of the king would see him through. If, on the other hand, the king were against him, then he could fall back on the support of Parliament. Only if the king and Parliament got together and ganged up on him did Pelham consider he was lost.[11]

Pelham's contemporary, Sir John Perceval, 1st Earl of Egmont, saw the relationship of king and Parliament in a rather less cynical but more confrontational light. Egmont wrote in his diary:

'Tis a solecism in our constitution to leave the same powers in the Crown which it had when more absolute, now that the subject has grown more powerful. . . . The king will say 'I won't or I will do this, and I insist on my prerogative' but Parliament will say 'Sir, you have the prerogative indeed, but 'tis an abuse of your prerogative and if insisted on, this matter in question will ruin us; therefore, if you are obstinate, we will distress you, you will have no supplies; you are ill advised . . .'[12]

The passage of time and the succession of George III, the first Hanoverian born and brought up in England, cleared up the paradox of a constitutional king who was also a despotic elector. George III, 22-year-old son of Prince Frederick, became king on the death of his grandfather, George II, in 1760. For a Hanoverian, the third George was unusual. For a start, he hated Hanover, which he called 'the horrid Electorate' and never visited. Unlike his two predecessors, he had no taste for mistresses. He was full of noble idealism and set out to be an exemplar of justice, honour and personal purity while seeing himself as the guardian of popular rights and liberties. 'The pride, the glory of Britain and the direct end of its constitution,' wrote the young George III, 'is political liberty.' The pioneers of constitutional monarchy some seventy years earlier could not have wished for a more complete statement of its principles. This, though, did not prevent King George III acquiring a completely different reputation in the early years of his very long reign: that of royal tyrant and closet despot plotting to subvert these same principles in Parliament and restore absolute monarchy to Britain.

This reputation came from two main sources. The first comprised the American colonists who fought, and won, their War of Independence from Britain in 1783 and demonised King George in the process. Puritans had been among the first English emigrants to settle in America after 1620 and they brought with them their view of monarchy as despotism. This concept filtered into the disputes which set off the bid for independence: taxation, the British government's right, which the colonists denied, to levy it, and the fact that they were not represented by their own members in Parliament.

King George's own view was that the revolution in America was treason, not only towards himself, but towards Parliament whose sovereignty he felt had been abused. This, in its turn, fed his obstinate determination to defeat the rebels. When he failed and the colonies won their independence as the United States, he was distraught, believing that he had betrayed his royal obligations – so much so that he contemplated abdication.

The second source that blackened the name – and the intentions – of George III was Edmund Burke, a Whig who put a different, but equally opprobrious, slant on the king's role in the War of Independence. He believed that but for the monarch's stubborn interference and incompetence, the war might never have occurred. Burke, a Dublin-born lawyer who first entered Parliament in 1766, was well known for advocating controversial causes: one was the emancipation of the Catholics which the king himself opposed, another, the government's policy in America, which Burke vehemently attacked.

Burke reserved his most savage barbs for the monarch and the monarchy, and King George's role in the decade of ministerial instability that followed his accession to the throne. In 1770, Burke published his *Thoughts on the Cause of the Present Discontent*, in which he purported to reveal a royal conspiracy to subvert Parliament and the constitutional monarchy.

First of all, Burke put forward a maverick view of the 'Glorious Revolution' of 1688 which had inaugurated the constitutional monarchy. The revolution had not served simply as a means of curtailing royal powers while allowing the monarch a limited role in government: constitutional monarchy, to Burke, was a way of prompting the king to step down from active politics and become a figurehead. In this scenario, any move the king might make to poke his head above the political parapet automatically appeared as an infringement of Parliament's rights. However, George III, a man of principle, refused to go along with Burke's ideas. He had every reason to stand by his powers under the constitution, which included the right to choose his own ministers and to use the Royal Assent, where he considered it necessary, to veto legislation.

King George never used the veto, but he was certainly involved in the choice of government ministers. His choices were not always successful: for example, Frederick, Lord North, the king's personal friend and his chief minister during the American War of Independence, lacked the temperament to manage such a major conflict and had to resign in 1782, the year before the war was finally lost.

Edmund Burke's conspiracy theory went a great deal deeper than this failure. He accused George III of gathering about him a group of 'King's Friends', most of them 'placemen' parked in Parliament to disrupt proceedings and destabilise the Commons. There was, Burke contended, a 'secret cabinet' in which this nefarious strategy was discussed, with the king's cooperation and connivance. Britain, Burke concluded, was in imminent danger of acquiring an absolute monarchy.

Burke's arguments were so influential that the royal 'conspiracy' remained on George III's record for almost 200 years. It was not until the first half of the twentieth century that the distinguished historian Sir Lewis Namier reassessed eighteenth-century politics in the light of King George's correspondence and the papers, discovered in around 1932, that had been left behind by his tutor, the Earl of Bute. Namier came to the conclusion that far from plotting a royal takeover of government, George III had no intention of arrogating total power to himself: he had acted, Namier stated, in defence of 'the vital interests and essential rights of the British nation'.[13]

If anything, the conspiracy was to be found in Burke's court rather than the king's. In 1765, just before he entered Parliament, Burke became private secretary to Charles Watson-Wentworth, 2nd Marquess of Rockingham, then first Lord of the Treasury. Rockingham found the fiery, eloquent Burke a useful mouthpiece for his own aim to curb the patronage exercised by the Crown. Rockingham was also strongly opposed to the war in America and, in fact, supported the independence of the colonies. He was, therefore, a natural choice to succeed the disgraced Frederick, Lord North, as chief minister in 1782. This was a disaster for the king, who detested Rockingham and all he stood for. Nevertheless, he had to swallow the return to power of the renegade marquess and the prospect of being sidelined by his government. All King George could do was bide his time and wait until the opportunity presented itself to get rid of the hated regime. Rockingham was well aware of the king's enmity, and of the difficulties his government would encounter if it lacked his backing. Attempts were therefore made to force support from the king by attacks on royal privileges. Of these, the Civil List Act, introduced into Parliament by Edmund Burke, was potentially the most discomfiting. It pruned the king's household, imposed economies on the monarchy and advocated that George III 'live of his own' by managing his income of £900,000 a year within the strict limits laid down by the Act. These restrictions, Burke believed, would bring the king to heel.[14]

It was a crucial misjudgement. Instead of giving in to the Whig upstarts who were trying to demolish his powers, George III came out fighting. He even attempted to influence junior ministers to wreck Burke's planned reforms. The attempt was discovered and halted, but it gave Rockingham and his ministry a frightening lesson in what royal power could do if sufficiently roused to defend itself. The lesson ended there, though. Rockingham died suddenly, at fifty-two, on 1 July 1782, after only fourteen weeks in office.

Even so, King George's problem was far from over. If anything, it grew worse. With Rockingham's death, the next in line was one of the marquess's secretaries of state, William Petty, 2nd Earl Shellburne. Shellburne's great personal enemy, Charles James Fox, had other ideas. In order to shut Shellburne out, Fox proposed that the cabinet should elect a new chief minister. The king turned that one down out of hand, so Fox tried a different tactic. He mended fences with another long-standing enemy, Frederick, Lord North, and on 4 April 1783, formed an alliance with him. The two of them manipulated William Cavendish Bentinck, 3rd Duke of Portland, into nominal leadership of their coalition and in 1783, King George was obliged to accept the package.

These were very dark days for the king. Not only did he detest the new government that had been foisted on him, he had been betrayed by his erstwhile friend, Lord North. Even worse than that, Charles James Fox was planning to curtail royal political power by transferring to the cabinet the king's right to appoint his own ministers. Fox saw that unless the king lost his right of appointment, Portland's ministry, which was anathema to him, could never be either stable or credible. King George was in despair. His entire *raison d'être* as a constitutional monarch was being whittled away. Once again he contemplated abdication. He wrote to his son, George, Prince of Wales:

> The situation of the times is such that I must, if I attempt to carry on the business of the nation, give up every political principle on which I have acted, which I should think very unjustifiable, as I have always attempted to act agreeable to my duty; and must form a ministry from among men who know I cannot trust them, and therefore will not accept office without making me a kind of slave.

Once more, though, the king rethought his position: when it came to the crunch, he was unable to desert his royal duty. Instead, George III used to the full those powers still left to him by refusing to grant noble titles to candidates proposed by the hated Portland ministry and giving places at court only to men on whom he could rely. For the rest, the king played possum, signing without complaint whatever papers ministers put in front of him, while waiting for a turn of events that could be to his advantage. He did not have to wait long.

Towards the end of 1783, Charles James Fox went too far: his East India Bill proposed making Parliament, not the Crown, responsible for appointing the governing commissioners in India. What was more, the Crown was not going to have the power to dismiss them. This was the king's opportunity and there was more to it than the obvious insult to himself: the East India Bill could be interpreted as an attempt by the Whigs to exploit India in order to keep themselves in office and also to enable Fox to acquire personal powers of patronage.

By this time, King George, at the age of forty-five, had been weathered by crises and had become a consummate politician in his own right. When controversy began to rumble over the East India Bill, he recognised his chance and took it. Stepping, for once, beyond the bounds of constitutional monarchy, he announced that any member of the House of Lords who voted for Fox's bill would be numbered among the enemies of the king.[15] This was not just emotional blackmail: the threat had its appeal to hard-headed materialism. No enemy of the king could receive royal patronage, lucrative offices and grants or any of the other favours the crown had at its disposal.

The East India Bill died the death and so did the cabinet that had introduced it. In the general election of December 1783, weakened by internal squabbles as well as by the king's initiative, Portland's Whig ministry was defeated. After decades in opposition, the Tories took power, led by the king's choice for chief minister, William Pitt the Younger, aged twenty-four. Charles James Fox refused to accept the vote that ousted him and until the day he died in 1806, he believed that the king had played a dastardly trick on him to ruin his political career.

Nevertheless, Fox had made an important contribution to British political life. Along with Edmund Burke and the Younger Pitt, he had introduced a new ingredient into the workings of Parliament and one that affected the constitutional monarchy: this was the arrival of the celebrity politician who would soon occupy centre stage and relegate the monarch to the wings. The process was greatly helped along by the emergence of the first national newspapers published in Britain. By this means, the cut and thrust of parliamentary debate, the personalities who took the floor, the speeches they made and the results of the vote made news stories that were eagerly absorbed and discussed in the coffee houses and inns. For the first time, politics became public property.

At the same time, royal news was more disturbing. George, Prince of Wales, the heir to the throne, was a rascally libertine and a profligate whose extravagance was such that he had to be bailed out twice by Parliament. More tragic was the porphyria which attacked King George in 1788 and was diagnosed as madness. Although his sanity was restored this time, the king never fully recovered, and in the end, the illness returned and destroyed him.

Long before this, though, the king's political input had faded away. George IV and William IV, the two sons who were his immediate successors, were not only unable to further the contribution their father had once made, they and their brothers brought the monarchy into disrepute. They majored in vice, scandal, corruption, indolence, womanising, and several other forms of excess. Not surprisingly, the royal family was mercilessly parodied by satirists, pamphleteers and cartoonists. Sir Arthur Wellesley, Duke of Wellington, was putting it mildly when he described the sons of George III as 'the damndest millstones about the neck of any government that can be imagined'.

In effect, the Royal Dukes, as the sons of George III were collectively known, had squandered the legacy of constitutional monarchy. Now, monarchs were no longer prime movers on the British political scene. At the same time, liberal reform was gathering pace and leaping ahead of their reactionary attitudes. Politically, the monarch was becoming irrelevant, for reforms took place and were enshrined in Acts of Parliament despite their opposition. George IV, for example, strongly opposed Catholic emancipation: yet the Catholic Emancipation Act was passed in 1829. Three years later, the Tories put up a fierce fight against the Great Reform Bill and William IV was right behind them. At one point in this very protracted process, the government had asked the king to create sufficient Whig peers to get the bill through the House of Lords: he attempted sabotage by refusing to create the number required for the purpose. Nevertheless, both the king and the Tories lost out. The Whigs triumphed and the Great Reform Bill, the first major reorganisation of Parliament to take place in nearly six centuries and a milestone on the path to democratic government, became law in 1832.

By this time, social as well as parliamentary reform was in the air and many once insurmountable barriers were coming down. With the abolition of slavery in 1833 and the Factory Acts of 1833, 1844 and 1847, Parliament attempted to redress decades of cruelty that had blighted the lives of millions. The push for universal suffrage, though not complete until 1928, gained impetus not only from the Great Reform Act but from its successors of 1867 and 1884. The spectrum of political power in Britain was widening, and the more extensive it grew, the less central the monarch became.

By the time Queen Victoria, the last of the Hanoverian monarchs, came to the throne in 1837, constitutional monarchy was fast becoming a synonym for the influential but powerless head of state whose place was above party and above politics. Victoria's husband, Prince Albert, may have given the royal family their role as social workers concerned with charity and the everyday lives of their subjects, but the area of operations once dominated by monarchs was a definite no-go area. This was sharply brought home to Victoria in 1880 when she made strenuous efforts to prevent the 72-year-old William Ewart Gladstone, whom she detested, from taking office as prime minister. The electorate, however, had spoken, and Victoria's favourite, Benjamin Disraeli, who flattered her outrageously, was defeated. Gladstone and the Liberal Party were in, and despite her antipathy, Victoria was forced to accept them. 'The Queen,' it was announced, 'does not the least care, but rather wishes it should be known that she has the greatest possible disinclination to take this half crazy and really in many ways ridiculous old man.'[16]

The ceremonial and pageantry remained, the deference royalty had always enjoyed was still there. Every aspect of national life bore the stamp of the monarch: for instance, the government was 'His or Her Majesty's government', 'Rex' – king – or 'Regina' – queen – brought cases for trial into the lawcourts. The real power, though, lay elsewhere, with the elected representatives in Parliament or the independent judges in the courts. However respectfully that had to be explained to Victoria's heir, King Edward VII, while the absolute monarchs of Europe looked on with a mixture of shock and contempt, it was then and remains today the *status quo* of British constitutional monarchy.

# NINE

## *Abolishing the Monarchy*

The abolition of monarchy is not a cataclysmic happening only because of the violence that frequently accompanies it. Normally, violence is simply the catalyst. What is really going on when monarchies fall by revolution is an endgame, the finishing touch to a process of change that has become inevitable.

The abolition of a monarchy may come about through an internal struggle in which discontented elements, often army officers, topple a monarch and take power. This accounts for the military coups that took place in Egypt in 1952, in Iraq in 1958, in Yemen in 1962, in Libya in 1969 and in Cambodia in 1970. In Afghanistan in 1973, the prime minister, Lieutenant-General Mohammed Daud Khan, set up a republic after deposing the king, Zahir Shah.

In 1975, King Savang Vatthana of Laos was forced to abdicate when communists took power: the king continued to live at the royal palace in Vientiane until 1977, when the authorities began to fear that he could act as a focus for popular discontent. Together with his queen, Khamboui, and the crown prince, Say Vongsavang, the king was snatched from the palace and was taken away by helicopter to a prison camp, Camp 01. The king and the crown prince died there in 1978, the queen in 1981. All of them were buried in unmarked graves outside the camp. The king, apparently, starved to death, but the then prime minister, later president, Kaysone Phomvihane, later gave the reason as old age. In Iran, in 1979, the shah, Mohamed Reza Pahlavi, was driven out of the country after his attempts to westernise his realm failed before the power of Islamists, led by Ayatollah Khomeini, who were intent on creating a theocracy ruled by the laws of Islam.

Although military intervention in politics has been a regular occurrence in regime change, it has not figured as the most common reason for the end of monarchy: that has been defeat at the hands of liberal revolutions intent on destroying the oligarchies that absolute monarchy has always typified. Even here, though, some countries have taken an alternative route – constitutional monarchy, a halfway house between absolute rule and republican rule, which retains the charisma of kings, yet at the same time caters for the democratic urges of their subjects. In Europe, Britain, Norway, Denmark, Sweden, the Netherlands, Belgium and Spain – since the restoration in 1975 – are all constitutional monarchies still operating on this basis in the twenty-first century.

Constitutional monarchy has also solved the problem of how to modernise the governance of countries where ancient beliefs about the divine nature of kings are still prevalent. In this scenario, removing the monarch could seem tantamount to blasphemy. The solution has been not to remove him, but convert him, as it were, into a more acceptable guise. This is what happened in Japan in 1945, when the Americans, victorious in the Second World War, realised that if they removed the emperor, Hirohito, chaos would follow: instead, Hirohito who was, reputedly, of divine descent, became a constitutional monarch.

A similar metamorphosis took place in Thailand in 1932 where the king, Prajadhipok, also known as Rama VII, was an absolute monarch, ruling by Divine Right. Then, on 24 June 1932, he received a telegram from the People's Party, a group of western-educated Thais who had just seized power. The telegram made him an irrefutable offer.

The People's Party consisting of civil and military officials have now taken over the administration of the country and have taken members of the Royal Family . . . as hostages. If members of the People's Party have received any injuries, the Princes held in pawn will suffer in consequence. The People's Party have no desire to make a seizure of the Royal possessions. . . . Their principal aim is to have a constitutional monarchy. We therefore invite Your

Majesty to return to the capital [Bangkok] to reign again as king under the constitutional monarchy as established by the People's Party. If your Majesty refuses to accept the offer or refrains from replying within one hour after the receipt of this message, the People's Party will proclaim the constitutional monarchical government by appointing another Prince whom they consider to be efficient to act as king.

King Prajadhipok had no option but to agree, but at least saved some 'face' by telling the rebels that he had already considered making the change to a constitutional monarchy himself.

Some sixty years later, in 1991, the late King Birendra of Nepal was in a similar position when political agitation in his small, poverty-stricken Himalayan kingdom grew so dangerous that he was forced, like Prajadhipok, to renounce absolutism and declare a constitutional monarchy. However, there was no question of deposing him: Birendra was considered to be the reincarnation of the Hindu god Vishnu, so that removing him would most likely have caused massive popular protest. For democratisation in Nepal to have any chance at all, the ancient religious tradition had to be upheld and Birendra, although updated as a monarch, had to remain in place.

Conditions in Europe did not afford kings the insurance of divinity. The Divine Right was the closest they came to it, but the Renaissance and its new spirit of enquiry eventually eroded unquestioning obedience to ancient traditions. Once that happened, established ideas and institutions, monarchy among them, came under critical scrutiny. The revival of ancient Greek and Roman culture that lay at the heart of the Renaissance provided a dramatic, if semi-legendary, example of what could happen when a liberty-loving people was confronted with a tyrant king. Lucius Tarquinius, known as Superbus or The Proud, arranged the assassination of his father-in-law and predecessor, Servius Tullius, to became the seventh and last king of Rome in 534 BC. Servius had been a moderate and had continued the tradition, long established in Rome, of consulting the senate on matters of policy. However, according to the Roman historian Titus Livius – Livy – the death of Servius 'marked the end of just and legitimate rule by kings in Rome'. Once Tarquin got his hands on power, he set out to be a despot.

In his *The Rise of Rome*, written five centuries after the event, Livy described what happened next:

> He killed off prominent senators who he believed had favoured Servius' interests. But then, realising that seizing the throne in the terrible way he did might set a precedent to be used against himself, he surrounded his person with an armed guard, for violent usurpation constituted his only claim to the throne, since he had received neither the vote of the people nor the consent of the senate. Worse still, because he . . . spread fear still further by trying people on capital charges in a court where no one save himself was the judge; under this charade, he was able to execute, exile and fine not just those he suspected or disliked, but those from whom he wanted nothing but their money.'[1]

The wealthy family of Lucius Junius Brutus were typical victims: after the death of Brutus's father, Tarquinius seized his property and killed his elder son. Brutus himself escaped only by feigning idiocy. The reign of Tarquinius, which was reputedly characterised by bloodshed and violence, was abruptly ended in 510 BC when his son Sextus added his own outrage to the family catalogue of abuses. He raped Lucretia, the wife of Tarquinius Collatinus, a Roman general, and she was so distraught at the disgrace that she killed herself.[2] Lucius Junius Brutus, longing to avenge himself on Tarquinius, roused the people of Rome to revolt, and together they drove out the king and his entire family. Tarquinius attempted several times to retrieve his throne, but failed and died in exile.

Meanwhile, the Roman monarchy was abolished and a republic was put in its place. However, the Romans had divested themselves of more than their kings. The very idea of kingship and royalty became anathema to them and in 55 BC, Julius Caesar was murdered on the suspicion that he intended to accept the crown. Subsequently, in 27 BC, Rome acquired the first of its emperors,

Augustus, Caesar's great-nephew. Neither he nor his successors used the imperial title or, worse still, called themselves kings. Instead, they took the title of *Princeps*, First Citizen, or *Pater Patriae*, Father of the Country.

Like so many tales from the ancient world, the story of Tarquinius Superbus contained a large element of legend and propaganda. Tarquinius appears as a typical Roman tyrant, complete with sinister intentions and dark deeds and a son who proved to be just as bad, if not worse, than his father. It is significant, nevertheless, that tyranny, as illustrated in this and other ancient history, was predicated on the denial of popular rights and the use of brute force and repression to keep the people in servitude. This concept made its contribution to Renaissance ideas of personal liberty and, most powerful of all, the claims to freedom of conscience that fuelled the Protestant Reformation.

The English Puritans, one of many splinter groups that afterwards went their own, strict Protestant way, emulated the Romans and identified kings and kingship with tyranny. As a result, they conducted, through Parliament, a civil war against their monarch, Charles I, that ended not only with his execution in 1649, but with the abolition of the monarchy in England.

The language used in Charles's indictment showed very clearly the connection the Puritans made between royalty and despotism. The king was charged with conceiving 'a wicked design to erect and uphold in himself an unlimited and tyrannical power to rule according to his Will, and to overthrow the Rights and Liberties of the People'. To this end, he 'traitorously and maliciously levied war against the present Parliament and the people therein represented', and [upheld] . . . a personal interest of Will and Power and pretended prerogative to himself and his family against the public interest, common right, liberty, justice and peace of the people of this nation.' Finally, he was impeached 'as a Tyrant, Traitor, Murderer, and a public and implacable Enemy to the Commonwealth of England'.

Sentiments like these found their echo in the revolt of the American colonies against the 'tyranny' of King George III after 1775. The ethos of the revolution and its emphasis on personal freedom owed a great deal to the Puritan view of monarchy, its privilege and its manipulative powers. This was spelled out in the Constitution of the United States which was adopted on 17 September 1787, four years after independence from Britain had been won. Section 9, Clause 8 reads: 'No Title of Nobility shall be granted by the United States: And no Person holding any Office of Profit or Trust under them, shall, without the Consent of the Congress, accept of any present, Emoluments, Office, or Title, of any kind whatever, from any King, Prince, or foreign State.'

This was not an item on its own, a precaution designed to stop individuals gaining personal aggrandisement at the expense of the state. Clause 8 was closely keyed in to a plan designed to prevent the development of monarchy or any other form of despotism in America and so keep the republic true to its principles. This was enshrined in a system of elected representation that was unique in its time. Under the US Constitution, there was to be no monopoly of power, as in a monarchy. Instead, government was shared between the president and Congress, which comprised the senate and the House of Representatives: this was intended to provide a balance of power that served as a check against tyranny.

The men who framed the American constitution were, of course, able to work in the vacuum created by throwing off the distant rule of King George III and the British Parliament. This was not a luxury available to the revolutionaries in France, who were mightily impressed by American ideals, but had to deal with the lumber, as they saw it, of centuries of absolute royal rule. Abolition of the monarchy was not, at first, included in French revolutionary plans. An early aim was to turn King Louis XVI into a British-style constitutional monarch with powers which he was required to share with the *parlements*, the lawcourts. The terrified Louis approved a new constitution containing these arrangements on 14 July 1790, a year to the day after the storming of the Bastille, but the mood in France was already moving beyond the point where constitutional monarchy was acceptable. The possibility vanished completely on 27 August 1791, when the prospect arose of a conspiracy by foreign monarchs to restore Louis to full royal autocratic authority in

France. At a meeting in Pillnitz in Prussia, Emperor Leopold II of Austria and the Prussian king, Frederick William II, invited other European monarchs to join them in attacking France.

This was, at first, seen as diplomatic manoeuvring rather than a serious call to arms: it was designed to pressurise the revolutionary Assembly and raise King Louis's hopes of rescue. It was, however, a dangerous game to play. In France, during 1791, three political clubs were planning the future of French government and two of them, the Jacobins and the Cordeliers, were in favour of a republic. The third, the Feuillants, led by the Marquis de Lafayette, opted for the new limited monarchy but they were isolated and outnumbered by the republicans when a new Legislative Assembly was formed on 1 October 1791.

At this juncture, interference by Prussia and Austria on behalf of King Louis and his family began to look much more serious. The Legislative Assembly received a stern warning that any move against the French royal family would be regarded as a signal for war. The Assembly's response to this threat was to declare war on Austria, on 20 April 1792. Fighting began at once along the frontier with Flanders. The French forces were quickly outclassed by the Austrians, who brushed them aside during skirmishes around the town of Lille. There was a pause in the hostilities as a large army, more than 152,000 men strong, assembled at Coblenz under the leadership of Karl Wilhelm, Duke of Brunswick. On 19 August, Brunswick invaded France and headed for Paris through the Argonne forest.

The attempt to rescue the French royal family was now putting them in even greater peril than before. The downfall of the monarchy had already occurred on 10 August 1792, when a Paris mob had broken into the Tuileries palace where they personally threatened the king. They forced him to don the red Phrygian cap, a symbol of the revolution, and drink a toast to their health and that of the French nation. Thoroughly frightened, the royal family looked to the Assembly to protect them, but they were asking in the wrong place. The republican majority in the Assembly, which re-formed as the National Convention and held its first meeting on 21 September, had placed the abolition of the monarchy at the top of the agenda.

There were scenes of great excitement which drowned out doubts about the legality of the move: much more acclaimed was a rabble-rousing statement from one delegate who demanded the destruction of 'this magic talisman. . . . Kings,' he said, 'are morally what monsters are physically.' The decree abolishing the monarchy in France was passed unanimously and the next day, 22 September, the establishment of the republic was announced. King Louis, now called plain Louis Capet, was put on trial, accused of treason. The indictment began: 'Louis, the French people accuses you of having committed a multitude of crimes in order to establish your tyranny by destroying its liberty.' Four months later, on 21 January 1793, King Louis was escorted by a guard of 1,200 horsemen to his place of execution. Henry Essex Edgeworth, an English priest, was with the king and later described the scene.

The streets were lined with citizens all armed, some with pikes and some with guns. . . . Nobody appeared either at the doors or windows, and in the street nothing was to be seen, but armed citizens – citizens, all rushing towards the commission of a crime.

The carriage proceeded . . . in silence to the Place de Louis XV, and stopped in the middle of a large space that had been left round the scaffold: this space was surrounded with cannon, and beyond, an armed multitude extended as far as the eye could reach. . . . As soon as the King left the carriage, three guards surrounded him, and would have taken off his clothes, but he repulsed them with haughtiness – he undressed himself, untied his neckcloth, opened his shirt, and arranged it himself. The guards, whom the determined countenance of the King had for a moment disconcerted, seemed to recover their audacity. They surrounded him again, and would have seized his hands. 'What are you attempting?' said the King, drawing back his hands. 'To bind you,' answered the wretches. 'To bind *me*,' said the King, with an indignant air. 'No! I shall never consent to that: do what you have been ordered, but you shall never bind me. . . .'

The path leading to the scaffold was extremely rough and difficult to pass; the King was obliged to lean on my arm, and from the slowness with which he proceeded, I feared for a moment that his courage might fail; but what was my astonishment, when arrived at the last step, I felt that he suddenly let go my arm, and I saw him cross with a firm foot the breadth of the whole scaffold . . . I heard him pronounce distinctly these memorable words: 'I die innocent of all the crimes laid to my charge; I Pardon those who have occasioned my death; and I pray to God that the blood you are going to shed may never be visited on France.'

A man on horseback, in the national uniform, and with a ferocious cry, ordered the drums to beat. Many voices were at the same time heard encouraging the executioners. They seemed reanimated themselves, in seizing with violence the most virtuous of Kings, they dragged him under the axe of the guillotine, which with one stroke severed his head from his body. All this passed in a moment. The youngest of the guards, who seemed about eighteen, immediately seized the head, and showed it to the people as he walked round the scaffold; he accompanied this monstrous ceremony with the most atrocious and indecent gestures. At first an awful silence prevailed; at length some cries of 'Vive la République!' were heard. By degrees the voices multiplied and in less than ten minutes this cry, a thousand times repeated, became the universal shout of the multitude, and every hat was in the air.

Shut away in the temple, the dead monarch's son, aged eight, became titular king of France as Louis XVII. Two years later he was dead, ostensibly of tuberculosis but more likely, as rumour had it, of poison. The same year, Revolutionary France acquired a new constitution. Better known as the 'Declaration of the Rights and the Duties of Man and the Citizen' it contained safeguards against the return of the monarchy. Article 17, for example, stated that 'Sovereignty lies primarily in the universality of the citizens' and Article 21 read 'Public office cannot become the property of those who exert it'.

Despite these precautions, the first French republic that was hailed with such enthusiasm did not live long. The three-man Directory set up by the 1795 constitution to govern France was soon hijacked by Napoleon Bonaparte: he crowned himself emperor eleven years after the death of Louis XVI. Even so, the philosophy of the French Revolution survived and proved seminal in the political development of nineteenth-century Europe. The liberal revolutions that sounded alarms across the continent throughout 1848 and into 1849 were one direct result of its legacy. Another was the advent of communism as outlined by the German theorist Karl Marx in his *Communist Manifesto*, published, appropriately enough, in 1848. With this, Marx lit a long, long fuse. Eventually, the explosions would reverberate over the next century, destroying several European monarchies along the way. None, however, went down in more dramatic fashion than the Romanov dynasty in Russia.

Romanov rule, which began in 1613 with the accession to the throne of Michael Romanov, had long been the epitome of repressive despotism. While the Renaissance was transforming the cultural life of western Europe, semi-oriental Russia was backward and barbaric. Despite the modernising efforts of Peter the Great in the seventeenth century or Catherine the Great in the eighteenth, the Russian aristocracy remained coarse and uncultured, and the peasantry, deeply poor, superstitious, illiterate and ignorant. Feudal serfdom survived in Russia longer than anywhere else in Europe: in 1800, half the Russian population of 90 million people were still serfs, bound like slaves to their aristocratic masters.

The liberal ideas of the eighteenth-century Enlightenment had proved startling enough in western Europe, where the Renaissance had at least prepared the ground and nurtured minds willing to contemplate political and social change. Russia, however, was so uncivilised that these same ideas landed there like bombshells. The tsars, accustomed to ruling by force and fear – the only way they thought their subjects understood – resorted to violent repressions. Even Catherine the Great, who had once flirted intellectually with liberalism, shed her interest after the French Revolution and imprisoned liberal thinkers or exiled them to the icy wastes of

Siberia. Tsar Nicholas I, who succeeded to the Russian throne in 1825, ruled by outright repression. He censored the Russian press, created a secret police force to hunt down liberals and revolutionaries and put down any unrest with the utmost cruelty. Nicholas's son and successor, Alexander II, attempted reforms, notably the freeing of the Russian serfs in 1861, the relaxation of press censorship and the introduction of more liberal education. All this encouraged educated Russians to demand more democracy and Alexander took fright. He reimposed repression, threw liberals out of the universities and had thousands of suspected revolutionaries sent to Siberia. This did not protect Alexander against the assassination plot that killed him in 1881, but it certainly fortified his successor, Alexander III, in his belief that liberal reform was futile and autocracy the only way to rule.

As the French had already discovered, autocracy was a practical proposition only if the ruler involved was a true despot, capable of forcing his will on his subjects. Once a weak monarch arrived with insufficient 'spine' to make repression stick, disaster was sure to follow. In this, late nineteenth- and early twentieth-century Russia saw a virtual repeat of the events, including the end of the monarchy, that occurred in France after the death of the mighty Louis XIV in 1715.

Nicholas II, son of Alexander III, was completely unsuited to be a despot. Mild-mannered, indecisive and of limited ability, he was well aware of his own shortcomings. He broke down in a lather of fear when his father's unexpected death pitchforked him on to the Russian throne in 1894. Nicholas was also the archetypal henpecked husband, dominated by his German wife Alexandra, a grand-daughter of Queen Victoria, who kept telling him to be strong. 'Never forget that you are and must remain autocratic emperor,' Alexandra wrote, '. . . show more power and decision. . . . Be Peter the Great, Ivan the Terrible, crush them all under you.'

Alexandra was wasting her time. A tsar so weak that he had to be told to act the autocrat was no autocrat. Instead, he was a gift to agitators who plotted ceaselessly against his government and to rioters, mutineers and any other rebels with a grievance. Like

Alexander II, Nicholas II attempted reforms, including the creation of a Duma or parliament, only to beat a hasty retreat back into repression when liberals and democrats took advantage and demanded more concessions. The secret police, the Okrana, were let loose on the troublemakers, who were hunted down, arrested and exiled to Siberia in their thousands.

Imperial repression, however, was no longer effective by the turn of the twentieth century. Now, there was a significant new element in the equation. Russia was in the process of industrial change and thousands of workers were streaming into the cotton, wool, iron and steel factories, forming groups which, unlike the supine Russian peasantry, could be roused to make political protests, go on strike and otherwise make big trouble for the tsarist government. Decades of cruelty, and the extreme poverty and squalor in which millions lived, the hopelessness and hardship of life in Russia – all these served to fuel the coming revolution to heights of hatred and violence unknown even to its bloodstained predecessor in eighteenth-century France.

The revolution, when it came, was carefully planned and prepared by the Social Democratic Workers' Party, formed in 1898. The Party leaders – Vladimir Ulyanov, known as Lenin, and Lev Bronstein, known as Trotsky, were both disciples of Karl Marx, and their purpose was to provoke a massive uprising that would rid Russia of the tsars and the tsarist monarchy once and for all. Initially, they were upstaged by the moderate Mensheviks, led by the liberal politician Aleksandr Fyodorovich Kerensky, who formed a provisional government in 1917 in order to democratise Russia. Lenin and Trotsky, however, had a much more fundamental, much more violent change in mind, and circumstances in Russia were far better suited to their agenda than to Kerensky's. In three punishing years of the First World War, the Russian armies had suffered devastating defeats and sustained more than five million casualties. As the war progressed, goods ran short and before long the people were starving. By March 1917, hungry workers were looting food shops.

With law, order and all control collapsing around them, liberals set up a provisional government on 12 March and together with the communist Soviet, demanded the abdication of Tsar Nicholas. Three days later, Nicholas resigned the throne, and wrote a bitter comment in his diary about the way the Russian Army had deserted him.

'In the morning,' the tsar wrote on 15 March, 'Ruzski [General Nikolai Ruzski, Commander of the Northern Army] came and read his very long direct-wire talk with Rodzianko [Chairman of the Duma]. According to this . . . my abdication is required . . . [General] Alexeev sent it on to all the commanders-in-chief. By two o'clock replies were received from them. The gist of them is that in order to save Russia and keep the army at the front quiet, such a step must be taken. I have agreed. . . . All around me there is treachery, cowardice, and deceit.'

The Romanov dynasty and the Russian monarchy were finished, although there was, at first, some hope that Tsar Nicholas and his family would survive and be allowed to go into exile. The circumstances of the war made this impossible. Several governments were approached but all of them refused to offer asylum. Tsar Nicholas, the autocrat, was *persona non grata*. Instead, the royal family was taken to the grimly named House of Special Purpose at Ekaterinburg deep inside Russia in the Ural Mountains. In mid-July 1918, word came that an army of White Russians – royalists opposed to the revolution – was approaching Ekaterinburg. The rescue of the royal family appeared imminent, but this was, in fact, their death warrant. On 18 July, Tsar Nicholas, his wife and all five of their children were executed by firing squad.[3]

In 1917, when the search was on for a place of asylum for the Romanovs, Nicholas's cousin, the English king, George V had been among those who declined to offer shelter. At the time, the king's precise reasons were not revealed. However, in his *War Memoirs* written in 1934, David Lloyd George, British prime minister during the First World War, cited two possible explanations: accepting the tsar and his family could have encouraged the republicans in Britain, and the British working class was hostile to a tsar who had caused so much grief and suffering to their counterparts in Russia.[4] This was, in its way, a sign of increasingly liberal times and of a new consciousness on the part of monarchs and politicians that *vox populi* was a voice they were obliged to heed.

That voice grew more and more insistent until it became a clamour that resulted in a virtual cull of monarchies during the first half of the twentieth century. The Russian, German, Austro-Hungarian and Ottoman crowns that ceased to exist after 1918 were the major headline casualties, but there were others, and it did not necessarily take a world war or similar catastrophe to bring them down. A liberal upsurge proved quite enough.

In 1910, nineteen-year-old King Manuel II of Portugal, who had come to the throne three years earlier, after his father and elder brother were assassinated, was ejected by a republican-led uprising. In Spain, the military dictatorship of Primo de Rivera collapsed in 1930 after seven years in power and his supporter, King Alfonso XIII, paid the price. Elections produced a huge republican majority in the Spanish parliament, the Cortes, and in 1931 Alfonso had no option but to leave the country. Nominally, he remained king, for he refused to abdicate but he never returned to Spain and died in exile in Rome in 1941.*

By this time, another world war was preparing the way for another generation of revolutionaries to overturn another batch of monarchies. The 'Iron Curtain' which, in Winston Churchill's vivid phrase, came down across Europe after 1945 turned several Balkan kingdoms into Russian communist satellites and resulted in banishment and exile for their monarchs. An early victim was King Peter II of Yugoslavia, who was deprived of his throne in 1945, when the communist guerrilla leader Josip Broz, better known as Marshal Tito, formally abolished the monarchy. King Peter never got over the shock, which overshadowed the rest of his life. His Greek wife, Queen Alexandra, whom he married in 1944, tried to convince him that he could never hope to retrieve his crown, but he

---

* The republic that replaced Alfonso XIII was defeated in the Spanish Civil War of 1936–9 by the Nationalists under General Francisco Franco. Although Franco subsequently became the dictator of Spain, officially the country remained a monarchy throughout his 36-year rule. Franco groomed Juan Carlos, grandson of Alfonso XIII, to take over from him. Juan Carlos became king of Spain after Franco's death in 1975.

refused to believe her and their marriage broke up over it. She went to live in Venice. Peter went to the United States where he became a pitiful figure, frequently drunk, and prone to regaling anyone and everyone with the great tragedy of his life and the beauties of Yugoslavia, which he never saw again. He never managed to restart his life, and failed dismally in attempts to set himself up as a consultant or a financier. By the time Peter reached his forties, he was a tired old man, bloated by drink, worn down by self-pity and broken by too much failure. Money ran short, and landlords, once impressed by having a royal tenant, began demanding their money. Hotels, likewise, were disinclined to let Peter through the doors. Peter died, aged only forty-seven, in 1970.

Another Balkan monarch, King Simeon II of Bulgaria, proved to be much more resilient and a great deal more enterprising. Simeon was only nine years old in 1946, when the communist People's Republic of Bulgaria abolished the monarchy and forced the child-king and his family into exile first in Egypt, afterwards in Spain. Simeon put his years in exile to positive use, obtaining a degree in law and political science and graduating as a second lieutenant from the prestigious Valley Forge Military Academy in the United States. Then, after fifty-five years in exile, he re-emerged in Bulgaria in a new guise, as Simeon Saxe-Coburg Gotha, political leader and head of the National Movement which won a landslide victory in parliamentary elections on 17 June 2001. The following 24 July, in a remarkable instance of how to turn adversity into triumph, the former king was sworn in as prime minister of the republic of Bulgaria.

This process was reversed by Zog I of Albania, who began life as a commoner and later made himself king. Ahmed Bey Zogu was head of a tribal clan in the Albanian highlands and when Albania became independent of Turkish rule in 1912, the seventeen-year-old Zogu took a blood oath to defend it. Ten years later, he came to power at the head of a republican government and converted himself into a king in 1928. Zog was, however, Albania's one and only monarch. He was forced out of the country in 1939 when the Italians invaded Albania and was never able to go back. The communist Enver Hoxha deposed him in 1946 and took power as prime minister: Hoxha's rule, which ruined the Albanian economy and left the country deep in poverty, lasted for forty years, until his death in 1985. King Zog had long since died, in 1961, and his son Leika became his nominal successor.

King Michael of Romania suffered a similar fate in 1947, when he was forced to abdicate. His kingdom was replaced by a people's republic, but Michael refused to go without a struggle. The king later recalled:

> I could not be responsible for a blood bath that would have cost so many innocent lives. . . . The Palace was surrounded by armed communist troops. The telephone lines had been cut. The Prime Minister, Petru Groza, had arrested a number of my staff. The thousand young people who were being held as hostages outside the Palace had been taking part in a demonstration against the communist regime. I refused several times to sign the documents. The Prime Minister let me feel his jacket pocket. He had a pistol. I had no choice.

Like Alfonso XIII of Spain, King Victor Emmanuel III of Italy made a very serious mistake that cost him the loyalty of his subjects and his throne: he gave his support to a brutal fascist dictator, Benito Mussolini, who bullied and terrified the diminutive monarch into accepting him as head of government in 1922. Mussolini's power ended towards the close of the Second World War in 1944, after the Allied invasion of Italy: he was murdered by Italian partisans in 1945. Victor Emmanuel survived the war, but in disgrace, and was forced to abdicate in 1946. He died in exile in Egypt the following year. Meanwhile, his son and successor, King Umberto II, enjoyed, if that is the word, one of the shortest reigns known to monarchy. Only five weeks passed between his accession and 13 June 1946, when Italians voted to abolish the monarchy and replace it with a republic.

By this time, republics, communist and otherwise, had made a virtual clean sweep of Europe. A fringe of constitutional monarchies remained in the north – the British, Belgian, Dutch, Norwegian,

Swedish and Danish – but there was only one survivor in the turbulent Balkans: Greece. Greece was one of five countries newly independent in the nineteenth century; the others were Belgium, Romania, Norway and Sweden, none of which had royal families of their own. Consequently, they imported kings from among the numerous princes, mainly German, who were going spare elsewhere in Europe.

The Greeks elected new monarchs twice, the first time in 1832 when they chose Otto of Bavaria: he proved militarily inept and his lack of an heir did not exactly please his macho Greek subjects. After Otto's forced abdication, the Greeks elected a second monarch, Prince William of Denmark, to replace him. William became King George I. Greece, however, had an evil reputation and not only because of the way Otto had been treated. It was a wild place, volcanic in its moods, and marked by a political life that broke records for venality, back-stabbing, corruption and barefaced treason. The unstable nature of his kingdom was not lost on King George, who, even at the age of eighteen, was canny enough to 'keep a portmanteau ready packed' in case he was forced to get out quickly and make a run for Denmark and home.

In the event, King George had no need of his portmanteau. He managed, sometimes barely, to survive for nearly forty years, although the savage nature of his adopted realm claimed him in the end: in 1912, he was assassinated by a mentally unbalanced tramp called Selinas who committed suicide before he could be brought to trial. George's descendants, however, had to use the portmanteau over and over again. It was no accident that ancient Greek drama so often dealt with elemental themes – death, retribution, ruin, expiation, disaster, exile – nor that the cast list usually consisted of royals. Some 2,500 years later, members of the royal family were still playing the same roles, as modern Greece proved to be the graveyard of monarchy. The Greek monarchy was abolished twice. Three kings were forced to abdicate, one of them on two occasions. The final *coup de grâce* came in 1967 when Greece, like so many other fallen monarchies, succumbed to a military coup. A *junta* of fascist colonels, led by George Papadopoulos, seized power and exiled the king, Constantine II. Constantine who had tried, but failed, to head off the coup, remained titular king of Greece until 1973, when the *junta* formally declared the monarchy at an end and proclaimed a republic. The following year, the *junta* collapsed and democratic government was restored – but not the monarchy. In a plebiscite, the Greeks voted against it, and for King Constantine and his family, their exile in London became permanent.

On the eve of the First World War, there were eighteen monarchies in Europe and only three republics – Switzerland which had never been ruled by kings, France and Portugal.[5] Six decades later, thirteen of those crowns* had disappeared. In 1991, after the collapse of the Soviet Union led to independence for its east European satellites, there was speculation that some, at least, of these lost monarchies were going to be restored. Similarly, in 2001, once the extreme Muslim government of the Taliban had been destroyed in Afghanistan in the wake of the terrorist attacks on the United States on 11 September, there was talk that the ex-king, Zahir Shah, by now eighty-six years old, was going to return. It made titillating newspaper copy, but it came to nothing. Governments might change, but republics remained. In Afghanistan, and across a vast swathe of Europe where crowns had once held sway and kings paraded in their splendour, the time for monarchy, it seems, was over.

---

\* Spain (nominally), Italy, Württemberg, Saxony, Bavaria, Germany, Austria-Hungary, Russia, Romania, Bulgaria, Greece, Montenegro, Serbia.

# TEN

## *The World of Royal Celebrities*

Kings, queens and royal families have always been celebrities. Historically, a great deal has always been expected of them. They have served as models of wisdom, mercy, justice and military prowess. They have typified patriotism and devotion to duty. They have set the pace in the arts and sciences. They have been regarded as exemplars of family virtues, the upholders of morality and decency, and generally speaking, as paradigms of all the virtues most valued in human society. This is a demanding agenda but royal celebrities have rarely been left to face the challenge 'warts and all'. Part of the necessary image is for royals to be larger than life, and for that purpose, inconvenient facts have usually been airbrushed out of the picture.

A case in point is the royal warrior-hero, whose deeds on the battlefield become the stuff of eulogy and legend, while their more mundane characteristics have been quietly buried in spin. For example, Richard I, the Lionheart, who became king of England in 1189 earned a celebrity that transcended the brutal realities of his life. Richard is still regarded today as the epitome of military excellence, a war leader of immense skill and a great Christian monarch. His main ambition after succeeding to the throne was to go on crusade to the Holy Land and he achieved it in 1191, when he became one of the leaders of the Third Crusade. The enterprise scored limited success: Richard relieved the Muslim siege of Acre and conquered a series of ports along the Mediterranean coast, but failed to achieve his main target, the capture of Jerusalem. Nevertheless, he had done enough to earn himself a glowing press in the chronicles of his time. These chronicles were written by the priests and other clerics who were usually the only literates of their

172

day. To them, there was no finer proof of Christian fidelity than leaving homeland, family and estates and risking life and health on the gruelling business of fighting the infidel in the Holy Land. Richard the Lionheart certainly qualified for celebrity on that score. As a result, the darker side of his character and reputation were played down for the sake of his heroic Christian image.

A discreet veil was drawn over Richard's probable homosexuality, even though this was anathema to the Church and was thought to bar perpetrators from going to Heaven. Likewise, his valiant image remained untarnished despite the nefarious means he used to raise the finance for his crusade. Richard cared little for England and spent only ten months of his ten-year reign in his kingdom which, for him, had only one purpose: to act as a treasure house for raising funds. To this end, Richard virtually put his realm up for sale: honours, licences, earldoms, lordships, sheriffdoms, castles, lands, estates, entire towns and anything else that could be turned into ready cash went to the highest bidders. Richard even planned to sell London, but as he complained, there was no one rich enough to buy it. Yet the kingdom he so signally neglected lionised the Lionheart to such an extent that he became one of its most famous royal celebrities, lauded in song, legend and film, and is today represented by a splendid equestrian statue that shows him outside the Houses of Parliament in London, clothed in armour, sword raised, ready for battle.

The Lionheart and other fighting heroes such as Edward, the Black Prince, or King Henry V, who also attained their celebrity on the battlefield, had an advantage not given to other royals whose fame had to be crafted outside the high drama of war. Courageous deeds and triumphs in battle earned ready-made celebrity and did so in a relatively short space of time. In 1346, for example, the Black Prince arrived at the battlefield of Crécy in France as an untried sixteen-year-old. In a little over two hours, he left it a charismatic hero with a reputation for prowess that lasted him a lifetime.

Similarly, Henry V, who became king of England in 1413, earned instant celebrity two years later with his victory over the French at the Battle of Agincourt. Agincourt, fought in northern France on 25 October 1415, made Henry's name as a warrior king through a circumstance long beloved of lore-makers: the English army of 8,900 men was vastly outnumbered by their French opponents who brought a force of around 30,000 to the battle. The English triumph therefore qualified as something of a miracle and miracles have always been excellent ground in which to sow the seeds of legend.

The warrior king as celebrity hero lasted only so long as the chief occupation of monarchs was war and Henry V belonged to one of the last generations to fill this role. Subsequently, war and fighting it became a matter for professional soldiers, and monarchs acquired celebrity from other sources. The dazzling Renaissance court was one of them. Another was the royal 'progress' in which monarchs travelled their realms to show themselves to their subjects, and while they were about it, impress them with their wealth and magnificence.

Opulent displays like these were a regular occurrence. For instance, a Tudor monarch arriving in London did so in splendour and at great expense. Triumphal arches were built, bonfires were burned, firework displays were staged, balconies were hung with rich materials to beautify the streets along which the monarch passed.[1] Although the age of knights in armour was long past when Henry VIII came to the English throne in 1509, he continued to use the knightly tournament as a public entertainment. It was an opportunity for more magnificence and more celebrity. In 1511 Henry spent £4,000 on a tournament at Westminster, twice as much as he spent on building his 900-ton warship the *Great Elizabeth*.

Henry VIII's younger daughter, Queen Elizabeth I, inherited her father's love of extravagant display and used it to create the glamorous image of herself as 'Gloriana'. Her court and courtiers were all part of the act as she created a legendary court carefully stage-managed by means of theatrical effects. Elizabeth was a great actress. Privately, she could be coarse and even foul-mouthed. She swore enormous oaths that made strong men blanch. She picked food from her teeth with a gold toothpick, never mind who was watching. She told bawdy jokes full of smut and innuendo. Yet, when occasion required, Elizabeth could be the epitome of royal dignity, 'of such a state in her carriage as every motion of her seemed to bear majesty.'[2]

Elizabeth's progress to church on Sunday was pure theatre. Lupold von Wedel, a Polish noble from Pomerania, was at the English court in 1584 and 1585, and described how the queen was preceded by guards carrying gilt halberds and dressed in 'red coats faced with black velvet in front and on the back . . . the Queen's arms'. The queen's privy councillors followed, two carrying the royal sceptre, another bearing the royal sword sheathed in a red velvet scabbard, embroidered with gold and set with precious stones and large pearls. The heralds were scarcely less flamboyant: they wore mantles of brilliant blue embroidered with wings. Eight trumpeters sounded a fanfare as Elizabeth passed by, two drummers produced rolls on their drums, and a piper played a melody.[3] This performance and other, similar displays at the court and during the queen's progresses perpetuated her fame so that even today, nearly five centuries after her life and reign, she remains one of England's greatest and most admired royal celebrities.

However, there was more to it than mere outward show. Like her father, Elizabeth I knew how to be a monarch, how to impose her personality on her court and how to guard against the over-familiarity that could break down the necessary distance between sovereign and subject. She might pose from time to time as a 'weak and feeble woman'. She might tease Devon-born Walter Raleigh about his broad West Country accent. She might nickname the Duc d'Alençon, her long time suitor, her 'frog', but none of it was an invitation to get closer to the queen than etiquette allowed. Simply talking to her was strictly governed by protocol.[4] A courtier summoned into the royal presence had to kneel while speaking – and even then only when spoken to – and remain kneeling until the queen told him he could rise. Leaving meant walking backwards, bowing twice before going through the door and out of sight.

Both King Henry VIII and his daughter knew how to preserve what a nineteenth-century economist and essayist, Walter Bagehot, called the 'royal mystique' and named as the essential ingredient for the survival of the monarchy. This, though, did not mean that monarchs always had to stand on their dignity or demand extreme shows of deference from their subjects. It was possible for a king to lead a riotous private life, yet retain respect and loyalty at a personal level. Charles II and Edward VII, for instance, often behaved outrageously but still managed to earn themselves the admiration and regard of their subjects. Though placed two centuries apart, the two kings had much in common. Both of them were immensely sociable and fun loving. Both kept a bevy of mistresses and sired several illegitimate children. Both possessed the 'common touch' which enabled them to communicate with anyone from the highest to the humblest and put all of them at their ease. Yet neither forgot for one moment who they were, and they expected everyone else to be aware of it, too.

In 1681, for example, Charles's appearance in full regalia at Oxford was an unmistakable statement of majesty, a piece of drama that abruptly ended the Exclusion Crisis. 'I will never yield,' Charles told the Whigs who had hoped to force the king to exclude his brother James from the succession, 'and I will not be intimidated.' This stern and awesome Charles proved immovable, but there was another, much more approachable Charles, the king who liked to walk his spaniels in London's St James's Park. Crowds would gather in the park to watch Charles feeding the ducks, playing games and talking to his mistress Nell Gwynn over the garden fence of the house he had given her in Pall Mall. The diarist John Evelyn witnessed the scene and was shocked to see the easy familiarity that existed between the king and 'Mrs Nelly', as he called her.

'I was heartily sorry at this scene,' Evelyn wrote in disapproval, only to be shocked again when King Charles moved on to another house that backed on to St James's Park – the house occupied by another of his mistresses, Barbara Villiers, the Duchess of Cleveland. John Evelyn was present again at the royal palace in 1685 when he observed 'the unexpressible luxury and profaneness . . . and dissolution' of Charles's court. The king himself sat 'toying with his mistresses'.

With an unreconstructed rake like Charles II on the throne of England, there was, of course, plenty to appal the priggish Evelyn and others, mainly Puritans, who were of like mind. However, a great part of Charles's popularity and his celebrity was based on the fact that he was no hypocrite. He had a roving eye and never bothered to conceal it. He loved bawdy Restoration plays with their suggestive dialogue and saucy interplay between the sexes and was frequently seen thoroughly enjoying himself at the theatre. This was the sort of king his subjects found it easy to like for being 'a bit of a lad'. In the end, even John Evelyn had to admit that Charles was 'a prince of many virtues . . . debonair, easy of access, not bloody or cruel . . . proper of person, every motion became him'.

The same could have been said of King Edward VII, another thoroughgoing philanderer who, even so, managed to combine royal dignity with friendliness and majesty with personal warmth. Leader of London high society, and an inveterate party-goer, Edward, who was known as Bertie in the royal family, was so convivial that his guests were sometimes tempted to relax too much and overstep the barriers. Once, during a weekend party at Sandringham, a female guest was so carried away by the jolly atmosphere that she addressed Bertie, then still Prince of Wales, as 'my good man'. The atmosphere froze at this piece of *lèse-majesté*. 'Please remember that I am not your good man,' the prince growled at her.[5]

Even those closest to him received the cold shoulder when they went too far. Bertie's mistress, the beautiful Lillie Langtry – the so-called Jersey Lily – once poured a handful of ice down the back of his neck as a joke during a costume ball. An awful silence ensued. The prince, his face black with fury, stared fixedly at Lillie for several seconds, then stalked from the room. From then on, Lillie Langtry was *persona non grata* in London high society and it took Bertie a long time to forgive her and take her back. What Lillie had forgotten in one mad, tomboy moment, was that the Prince of Wales was very conscious of his royal dignity and that no one, not even the famed Jersey Lily, could make him look foolish in public and get away with it.

Edward, on the other hand, consistently 'got away with it' because high society and the press conspired together to protect him from the scandals he himself created. Gossip knew all about Bertie's flamboyant way of life, but it was 'not done' to talk openly about it. A deferential press ensured that the royal escapades never became official public knowledge and in country houses where Edward and his current mistress stayed at weekends, the situation was acknowledged, but never spelled out. Instead, the couple were quietly given adjoining rooms.

Mistresses – so many of them that Bertie probably lost count – were only one aspect of a life which involved almost every sin and solecism known to Victorian society. Bertie drank, smoked, feasted and gambled, all to excess. When he was abroad, he frequented the brothels of Paris and hunted fresh game at Marienbad and other spas where hordes of women, from society ladies to courtesans, were there for the picking. Virtually everything he did horrified prudish Victorian society, all the more so when the inevitable occurred and his philandering involved him in high-profile scandal. In 1870, he came close to being cited as a co-respondent in the controversial Mordaunt divorce. Scandal was averted and the prince escaped cross-examination when Lady Mordaunt was declared insane, but six years later he was named as a potential witness in another high society divorce.

In 1890, Edward caused a fresh furore when he was involved in a messy court wrangle after his partner at an illegal game of baccarat at Tranby Croft in Yorkshire was accused of cheating. Cheating at cards was the ultimate solecism in Victorian high society and the scandal reached its climax when Edward appeared in the witness box at the trial. Members of the royal family, most particularly the heir to the throne, were supposed to be proof against such public exposure. Instead, there was talk that he had disgraced his mother, Queen Victoria, and the entire royal family and that he was not fit to inherit the throne. The French press, which was not under the same restraints as its British counter-part, freely speculated that Bertie was going to give up his right to succeed.

However, what the French and Bertie's other critics had forgotten was that in itself, royal immorality had never wrecked the prospects of an heir to the English throne. However much the prudes and Puritans disapproved of Bertie, there was an undertow of popular feeling that, like Charles II, he was simply doing what came naturally to a red-blooded man and that whatever boundaries of behaviour he overstepped, he was not vicious nor was he disloyal to the crown, its traditions and its dignity. It followed that moral lapses could be forgiven, but dereliction of royal duty, never.

It was by forgetting this golden rule that Edward VII's grandson, Edward VIII, one of the most glamorous royal celebrities of modern times, learned just how far it was possible for a prince and king to fall from grace. Known as David in the royal family, Edward, as Prince of Wales, was one of the most popular royals England ever produced. He had an extraordinary ability to 'connect' with ordinary people, and on his numerous tours abroad he proved himself a real charmer, with an engaging manner, a dazzling smile and the boyish good looks of a film star. This, though, was not what was required of a future king of England: in the early twentieth century, which had not yet slipped the bonds of Victorian respectability, the heir to the throne needed to be much more staid and dignified.

Just as undesirable was David's chosen lifestyle. Instead of the 'approved' families of impeccable lineage and reputation preferred by his parents, King George V and Queen Mary, David preferred to mix with social climbers, *nouveaux-riches* and sundry shady characters who inhabited the *demi-monde* that existed on the fringes of respectable society. It was in this 'half world', in 1930, that David first met and before long fell in love with Mrs Wallis Simpson, an American living in London with her second husband, Ernest.

David came to the throne as King Edward VIII on the death of his father at the beginning of 1936. From the start, he was determined to marry Wallis, after her divorce from Ernest, and make her his queen. The new king faced formidable opposition from the start. Ranged against him were the governments of Britain and the dominions – Australia, New Zealand, Canada, South Africa – the Church and the royal family itself. To all of them, marriage to Wallis Simpson was anathema not because she was an American, but because she was a divorcee with two husbands still living. At this time, divorce was not respectable and divorcees were socially undesirable: they were not allowed to mix with royalty, let alone marry into their exalted ranks.

The question of the king's marriage grew to crisis proportions throughout 1936. Although the foreign press was full of the story, their counterparts in Britain maintained a voluntary silence on the matter. In the days before television, the intrusive modern media and widespread foreign travel out of Britain, it was possible to keep a secret from the mass of King Edward's subjects, even a secret of these proportions. This, though, made the shock all the worse when the truth was at last revealed in the British press on 3 December. Eight days later, faced with a stark choice – Wallis or the Crown – the king chose Wallis and abdicated.

Edward had his supporters. Winston Churchill, for example, believed that he should be allowed 'his little bit of fluff', but far stronger and more vociferous was the public reaction which, on a personal level, compared closely to being jilted. There was fury, grief, contempt and bewilderment. Edward VIII was not the first king of England to resign his crown, but he was the first to do so voluntarily. This went completely against something the British public had long taken for granted: the personal sacrifice monarchs were expected to make for the sake of their birthright. However unreasonable, however selfish that was, it was something Edward, to his cost, had failed to take into account. He had just discovered that his celebrity counted for nothing once he refused to pay the price of royal duty.

His punishment was lifelong. The ex-king and Mrs Simpson married in 1937, but, as Duke and Duchess of Windsor, their life together was one of notoriety and exile. The loss of royal dignity was complete. The Windsors featured in newspaper gossip columns as social butterflies with too much time and money on their hands, flitting from one empty amusement to the next. They were the target for salacious gossip, including speculation that the duchess was unable to function as a normal wife because she was a hermaphrodite – part man, part woman. The Windsors were never officially accepted by the British royal family, the government or the Establishment. The duke was never forgiven for deserting his post and the duchess was never accorded the title 'Her Royal Highness' which he coveted on her behalf. He died in 1972, and the duchess in 1986.

By that time, social attitudes towards the monarchy and to morality in general had moved on, to arrive at a paradox. The so-called 'permissive society' had outlived the 'swinging sixties' that produced it and created what some might call a new decadence; attitudes were now more relaxed when it came to divorce, remarriage, cohabitation, illegitimacy or extra-marital affairs. Yet, at the same time, royalty was popularly supposed to maintain traditional standards, as exemplars of respectability, free from the taint of moral wrongdoing. It gave an entirely new meaning to the old adage that there was one law for the rich and another for the poor.

In 2000 and 2001, this paradox was seen at work in Norway, where public opinion was in ferment over the love life of the heir to the throne, Crown Prince Haakon. The story first broke in May 2000, when scandal looked likely over Haakon's romance with Mette-Marit Tjessem Høiby, an unmarried mother who had a child from a former relationship with a man convicted of possessing drugs. Before long, the affair was scaling the heights of constitutional crisis. The prince and Mette-Marit made no secret of their intention to live together and although this was a common-place arrangement in Norway, there was a strong public feeling that royals should be exceptions to the rule. Norwegians, it seems, believed that royals living with or marrying commoners made the monarchy appear 'too ordinary'. This conclusion was backed up by adverse reaction to the romance between Princess Martha Louise, Crown Prince Haakon's elder sister, and Danish author Ari Behn, whose connections with the drug world had made him controversial.

Support for the monarchy managed to hang on, although it only just squeezed through in one poll, where the Norwegian royals scored a 59 per cent approval rating. This, though, had no effect on anti-monarchists in Norway. The Liberal and Labour parties and the Christian Democrats in the *Storting*, the Norwegian parliament, called for an end to the monarchy in favour of a republic.

In March 2001, just after the crown prince's wedding plans were announced, a pressure group in Kirkenes, in north-east Norway, went public with a campaign aimed at dethroning the royal family. They even suggested that on the wedding day, 25 August 2001,

Norwegians should leave the country in protest. None of this prevented the royal wedding from taking place. Crown Prince Haakon and Mette-Marit were duly married on the appointed day at the Domkirken, the cathedral in Oslo, which had been refurbished specially for the occasion. Princess Martha-Louise and Ari Behn were married on 24 May 2002.

The furore over the romances in the Norwegian royal family was not only about the resurfacing of traditional views on royal behaviour. What was also involved here was a new slant on the whole business of celebrity and living with celebrity. It had become much more public. The days when the media would keep quiet about the illicit affairs of King Edward VII or the makings of the constitutional crisis of 1936 were gone forever once it became possible to deploy freedom of thought, opinion, speech and action on an almost unlimited scale. Egged on by a rampant, intrusive tabloid press specialising in sensational exposés, public opinion – on monarchy or anything else – became more vociferous than ever before.

The effect this could have on the standing of monarchy and how vulnerable royalty could be to adverse public opinion was illustrated by the sad story of King Leopold III of Belgium. In 1935, when the press in Europe was already claiming unprecedented rights of comment and expression, Leopold was widely blamed for causing the death of his wife, the beautiful and very popular Queen Astrid. The queen died in a car crash in Switzerland. Her husband was driving.

Leopold's reputation never recovered. After Nazi German forces invaded Belgium in 1940, during the Second World War, Leopold was accused of treason for making a hasty peace with the invaders. The Belgian public, burdened with Nazi occupation for the next four years, reacted with fury when it was learned that King Leopold had remarried in 1941 while a prisoner of war in Laeken Castle. Leopold's second wife, Marie Liliane Baels, a commoner, never became queen, though the king gave her the courtesy title of Princess de Réthy. Following the D-Day invasions of 1944, King Leopold and his family were removed to Germany, where they were released by Allied troops in 1945. Although he had never actively cooperated with the Nazi occupiers during the war, popular feeling against Leopold was so great that he was forbidden to return to Belgium without the permission of Parliament. In complete contrast, in the first heady days of liberation in 1945, the king of Norway, Haakon VII, and Denmark, Christian X, both of whom had been revered symbols of resistance to the Nazi invaders, were hailed as heroes of the hour.

A chance of acceptance, if not the emotional welcome given to Haakon and Christian, was offered to Leopold by a referendum held in 1950. Belgians voted narrowly for his restoration, and after Parliament authorised Leopold's return, he arrived in Brussels ready to assume his crown once again. The vote, however, had been too narrow. Leopold was greeted by strikes and demonstrations. Belgium's socialist government resigned in protest and there were violent clashes between police and anti-Leopold crowds. Clearly, it would be impossible for the king to resume royal powers, and on 16 July 1951 he abdicated in favour of his eldest son, Prince Baudouin.

Meanwhile, in the neighbouring Netherlands, Queen Juliana crossed swords several times with outraged public opinion. She first came under serious attack after 1952, when she called in a sham faith healer, Grete Hofmans, to save the eyesight of her youngest daughter, Princess Marijka. Hofmans, a devout pacifist who also believed that aliens had invaded Earth, did much more than tend the young princess. She influenced Juliana's political views and it was through her that the queen became opposed to important military alliances, such as the North Atlantic Treaty Organisation. The resultant scandal was not quietened until Juliana at last pulled back from the brink by dismissing Hofmans and forcing her to leave her apartment at the Soestdijk Palace.

Subsequently, the marriages of two of Juliana's daughters caused sensations in the Netherlands. In 1963, Princess Irene converted to Catholicism and, without permission, married Carlos Hugo, pretender to the Spanish throne and a leader of Spain's fascist party. In 1965, Juliana's heir, Princess Beatrix, announced her engagement to a German diplomat, Claus von Amsberg, who had once been a member of the Hitler Youth and fought with the German

*Wehrmacht*, the army, in the Second World War. Angry demonstrators took to the streets, proclaiming the marriage an act of treason. Predictions were made that this was the end of the monarchy. The marriage took place nevertheless, in 1966. The following year, the birth of a prince, Willem-Alexander, the first male heir to the Dutch throne for over a century, cooled the criticism.

This, though, was not the end of scandals for the Dutch House of Orange: in 1976, it was revealed that Queen Juliana's husband, Prince Bernhard, had accepted a $1.1 million bribe from the Lockheed Corporation to influence the Dutch government to buy its fighter aircraft. Like the Grete Hofmans affair, the Lockheed scandal cast doubts on the credibility of the Dutch monarchy. It was widely believed to have influenced Juliana's decision in 1980 to abdicate in favour of Beatrix. Even so, anti-monarchy sentiment ran at such a pitch that there were riots on 30 April, the day Queen Beatrix's coronation took place.

Beatrix veered close to scandal yet again over the marriage of her own heir, Prince Willem-Alexander, to an Argentinian, Maxima Zorrieguita, early in 2002. Maxima's father was the cause of the trouble: Jorge Zorrieguita had been a government minister during Jorge Videla's brutal dictatorship in Argentina between 1976 and 1981. Another royal marriage, it seemed, was heading for controversy, but the day was saved when Señor Zorrieguita agreed to a considerable sacrifice for a proud father: he stayed away from his daughter's wedding which took place on 2 February 2002.

In the first years after the Second World War, while the Belgian and Dutch monarchies confronted headline problems and their end was regularly prophesied, members of the British royal family remained relatively low-key celebrities. King George VI, brother and successor of Edward VIII, and Queen Elizabeth, the late Queen Mother, were largely responsible for restoring public faith in the monarchy after the trauma of the abdication. King George, a nervous monarch with a pronounced stammer and no training or inclination for the throne, earned much public sympathy for his plight and admiration for the way in which he had tackled his unexpected task. The role played by both the king and queen during the war when they regularly toured bombed-out areas and sympathised with the homeless, increased their reputation as exemplars of duty and social leadership. Meanwhile, at home, they built up an image of a happy, united royal family. They were, it seemed, secure on the pedestal of public esteem.

The atmosphere began to change, however, after the death of King George in 1952. Gradually, the British press became less deferential and more prone to speculation about royal private lives. Unfortunately, the royal family provided them with targets. There was, first of all, the doomed romance between Princess Margaret, the sister of Queen Elizabeth II, and a divorced man, the royal equerry Group Captain Peter Townsend. Margaret was pressurised to give up this 'unsuitable' match and it ended with a public statement in 1955 that she had decided not to marry Townsend. This, though, was not the end of it. The vast amount of personal publicity and speculation lavished by the press on the Townsend affair seemed to open the way to a less respectful, less restrained press treatment of the monarchy.

Unfortunately, intrusions into the lives of royal celebrities were enabled, rather than diverted, by the royal family's practice of keeping silent on controversial media stories. This was supposed to prevent their becoming embroiled in unseemly public arguments, but it also left the media free to speculate and gossip in the knowledge that, in the main, the monarchy never sued. It was partly to counteract this tendency and show the real life led by the queen, her husband and her four children, that a two-hour television programme, *The Royal Family* was made in 1969. Aired on 21 June, the film showed the royal family as they had never been seen before – off duty, eating meals, relaxing at home, chatting and joking together.

For the viewing public, this was a revelation. Although there had always been an impression of accessibility, public appearances by members of the royal family were, in reality, carefully stage-managed to appear relaxed and casual. Behind this façade, royals smiled and waved, but the royal mystique was preserved by keeping public curiosity at a discreet distance. Information, such as it was, remained strictly controlled. During the Second World War, for example, newsreels showing footage of the then Princess Elizabeth were monitored before they were allowed to appear on cinema screens. Until 1948, there was no court correspondent reporting on official royal engagements on radio. In 1953, a proposal to televise the coronation of Queen Elizabeth II was turned down flat by officials in charge of arrangements at Buckingham Palace: the ceremony was televised only at the insistence of the queen herself.

At this stage, the press and the public appeared to believe that the monarchy and the royal family, most particularly the queen, were above criticism and that only a thoroughgoing cad would breathe a word against them. In 1957, the 'cad' made his appearance in the person of John Grigg, Lord Altrincham, who was pilloried for publishing an article in which he called the monarchy 'complacent' and 'out of touch'. Altrincham also accused the queen of being elitist and of speaking like a gawky schoolgirl. Punishment was both swift and savage. Altrincham's radio and other professional engagements were cancelled. He was thrown out of his clubs. After he was interviewed on television, a man from the studio audience came up and hit him in the face. As for the national press, they went into a lather of fury at the very idea that the queen should be personally criticised.

Just twelve years later, after *The Royal Family* was filmed, this approach was consigned to the reverential past. For the film had the opposite effect to the one intended. Far from dissipating speculation and gossip, it opened the door to a brand of intrusion never before imagined. Now it was open season on the royal family and one of the first targets, once again, was Princess Margaret. In 1973, press cameramen followed her to the Caribbean island of Mustique and photographed her with her friend, the much younger Roddy Llewellyn. By 1978, the year Margaret and her husband, Anthony Armstrong-Jones, Lord Snowdon, were divorced, newspapers were hounding the princess, demanding that she choose between Roddy and her royal duties. Margaret was labelled 'lazy' and 'decadent': it was the first time a member of the royal family had been attacked in this insulting fashion but it was by no means the last.

The day the full weight of press interest at its most avid fell on the royal family was 24 February 1981, when the engagement of Prince Charles to the shy, diffident nineteen-year-old Lady Diana Spencer was announced at Buckingham Palace. From then on, Lady Diana was relentlessly tracked, pursued and photographed. Her wedding to Charles on 29 July was watched by 750 million television viewers worldwide and from then on, the new Princess of Wales was the most familiar face to appear in newspapers and magazines. More than that, her face actually sold magazines: all she had to do was appear on the front cover.

The British press and the people had waited a long time for someone like Diana to appear on the royal scene. So, too, had the fashion world, which longed for a royal role model for many years and were soon to turn the tall, slim, blonde princess into the greatest style icon ever known to British royalty. Princesses of Wales had always been a particular focus of interest. They were queens-in-waiting, and were therefore more accessible and approachable than they would one day become when their husbands ascended the throne and the consort's title was theirs. With no basic function apart from the duty to produce heirs to the throne, Princesses of Wales were free to make their own royal way and craft the role that best suited them. Diana's most famous predecessor, Alexandra of Denmark, wife of the future King Edward VII, was adored by the Victorian public for her beauty, her grace, her charity and her fortitude in putting up with the extra-marital antics of her libertine husband.

Diana, however, possessed an added advantage: Alexandra had been royalty, a Danish princess, but Diana, though the daughter of an earl, was a commoner and that made her seem closer to ordinary people than royals could normally manage. Added to that, Diana had an unusual ability to make herself appear like 'the girl next door', everyone's daughter or sister and, after the births of her two sons, a mother who could chat with all other mothers on an equal basis. During public engagements, no emotional holds were barred. Diana specialised in what came to be known as the 'touchy-feely' approach with public kisses and cuddles for toddlers or heart-to-heart exchanges with members of the public who flocked to see her. This added a facet to Diana's celebrity no other royal had ever matched.

It was not, however, the sort of celebrity that normally accrued to members of the British royal family. It was much closer to the type of fame courted by rock, television or film stars, full of dazzle and glamour – of lives lived in the searchlight of publicity. It was designed to attract love and excitement, fan-style emotion rather than loyalty or respect, and did nothing to impress with royal dignity. All the same, the public, both at home and abroad, loved the Diana approach and warmed enthusiastically to her charity work, her compassion for the poor and downtrodden, her love for her two sons, William and Harry, in fact to anything and everything about her. Before long, Diana's popularity soared to such heights that it began to eclipse that of all other British royals except, perhaps, the late Queen Elizabeth, the Queen Mother.

With this, a subtle change came over the public's perception of the British royal family. Once, a certain stateliness, an air of majesty had been appreciated in royalty. This, it was supposed, was how royalty was meant to be. However, after Diana came along with a much more emotional approach, this distant grandeur began to look stiff and unfeeling, and the royal refusal to respond to the tales the media told about them looked like arrogance.

The advantage of royal 'distance' and the dangers of 'letting it all hang out', Diana-style, soon became apparent as her marriage to Prince Charles ran into serious trouble. At the start, in 1981, the press had erected the sentimental edifice of the 'fairytale marriage'. However, as early as 1982, the media was already hinting at trouble in the Wales household, and ten years later, when the marriage was falling apart, the urge to tear down what they had built up took over with a vengeance. As a result, Charles and Diana were given no chance to handle the matter the old-fashioned way: withdraw behind a screen of discretion, settle their differences in private and so preserve face. Instead, the whole drama was played out in the full glare of headline sensations, lurid revelations, speculation and the release of intimate conversations on tape in which both Charles and Diana featured talking to their lovers. The coverage ventured so deeply into questionable taste that, in 1992, Buckingham Palace asked the Press Complaints Commission to issue a condemnation. It read:

> The recent intrusive and speculative treatment by sections of the press and indeed by broadcasters of the marriage of the Prince and Princess of Wales is an odious exhibition of journalists dabbling their fingers into the stuff of other people's souls . . .

One important factor not specifically mentioned was the publication in 1992 of *Diana, Her True Story* by Andrew Morton. This sensational, 'tell-all' book was a counterblast to several sentimental accounts that had marked the tenth anniversary of the royal wedding in 1991. Morton's book was a one-sided view – Diana's view – but it was dynamite: it traced the agonies of a crumbling relationship, the 'three in a marriage' situation with Charles's mistress, Camilla Parker-Bowles, and the eating disorders and suicide attempts of the lonely, neglected princess as she suffered at the hands of an indifferent husband and his hostile and insensitive family. At the time, there were strong denials that Diana had anything to do with the book, even though it was evident that only she could have known about the anatomy of her doomed marriage in such intimate detail. It was later revealed, after her death in 1997, that she had given Morton her full cooperation.

However, five years earlier, *Diana, Her True Story* served to make Prince Charles so unpopular that his right to succeed to the throne was questioned in the press and the survival of the monarchy itself was put in doubt. The book was also the catalyst that finally prompted the separation of the royal couple and laid the ground for their divorce in 1996. The high-profile divorce of the heir to the throne, especially when acted out in the blaze of press publicity, was new and untried ground. The British monarchy, though, had encountered crises many times before and its toughness and resilience soon kicked in to dissipate the idea, openly promoted in the media, that Diana was about to topple the House of Windsor. With this, the expectations raised by the press proved to be so much hot air. For example, the idea was floated that Diana was calling the shots in the divorce negotiations and making demands that a hapless royal family would have to grant her. In the event, the royal Establishment had no interest in Diana's celebrity or in the sympathetic press she received: the major figure to be preserved was the rightful heir to the throne, which was why the royal ranks closed about Prince Charles and left Diana out in the cold. For the same reason, Diana was stripped of the title 'Her Royal Highness' and her personal bodyguards were removed once the divorce came through and she was no longer a member of the royal family. Subsequently, against all predictions to the contrary, the reputation of the queen and her family revived and talk of denying Charles the throne, once so vociferous, faded away.

After her sudden death in a Paris car crash in 1997, the Diana legend seemed about to revive on a wave of high emotion verging on hysteria, but this, too, proved ephemeral. Within a year, there were admissions in the press that reporters and cameramen moving among the crowds that converged on London in the week before Diana's funeral had concentrated on the most tearful scenes of grief; this gave a misleading impression that the whole of Britain was shell-shocked and deep in mourning. In time, Diana's fame, which had once appeared so overwhelming, faded from the coverage that had once so avidly promoted it. It revived only when some matter connected with her became news, such as the trial in 2002 of her butler, Paul Burrell. Burrell was accused of stealing from Diana, Prince Charles and Prince William, but he was dramatically acquitted when the proceedings were halted after the queen furnished evidence exonerating him. Once the story was over, though, Diana once more disappeared from the headlines.

This made a cogent point about those monarchies, in Britain and elsewhere, which have beaten the republican odds to persist in a democratic world. Powerful publicity machines may create controversy and sensation, build up celebrities, tear them down and repeat the exercise with someone else, but their credentials are no match for monarchy which is backed by history, tradition, religion, philosophy and a very long acquaintance with survival.

# Notes

## Chapter One

1. Nicolson, p. 13.
2. Ibid., p. 14.
3. Frazer (*Lectures*), pp. 84–5.
4. Frazer (*Golden Bough*), p. 228.
5. Ibid., pp. 232–3.
6. Lewis, (*The Aztecs*), pp. 62–3.
7. Exodus 20: 2–4.
8. 1 Samuel 28: 15–19.
9. 2 Samuel 8: 2–5.
10. Exodus 34: 12/15–16.

## Chapter Two

1. Nicolson, p. 17.
2. Kautilya, Book 1, ch. 7.
3. Ibid., Book 1, ch. 19.
4. Mazumdar, pp. 111–14.
5. James, p. 5.
6. Kershaw, pp. 186–7.
7. Ibid., pp. 28, 31–2.
8. Milton, Samurai William, p. 20.
9. Packard, pp. 142–3.
10. Ibid., p. 145.
11. Ibid., p. 217.
12. Paludan, p. 203.
13. Lewis (*Ritual Sacrifice*), pp. 140–3.
14. Paludan, p. 192.

## Chapter Three

1. Exodus 20: 105.
2. Nicolson, pp. 305 ff.
3. Lewis (*Ritual Sacrifice*), pp. 65 ff.
4. Ibid., pp. 65 ff.
5. Nicolson, pp. 141–2.
6. Wood, p. 8 ff.

## Chapter Four

1. Richardson, p. 48.
2. Adamson, pp. 30–1.
3. Ibid., pp. 31, 104–5.
4. Ibid., p. 31.

## Chapter Five

1. Richardson, p. 104.
2. Church, p. 196.
3. Erlanger, p. 109.
4. Ibid., p. 117.
5. Ibid., p. 110.
6. Ibid., p. 111.
7. Adamson, p. 88.
8. Erlanger, p. 119.

# Notes

## Chapter Six

1. Barker, pp. 22–3.
2. Price, p. 41.
3. Ibid., p. 23.
4. Ibid., p. 40.
5. Ibid., p. 38.

## Chapter Seven

1. Lander, p. 7.
2. Ibid., p. 10.
3. Ibid., p. 11.
4. 1 Samuel: 16, 24, 26 and 2 Samuel: 1, 19.
5. Black, p. 457 n. 1.
6. Ibid., pp. 194–5.
7. Davies, p. 70.

## Chapter Eight

1. Rose, p. 224.
2. Ibid., pp. 176–7.
3. Zeigler, p. 60.
4. Clark, p. 252.
5. Ibid., p. 253.
6. Hatton, pp. 105–9.

7. Williams, pp. 14–15.
8. Ibid., pp. 15–16.
9. Ibid., pp. 16–17.
10. Ibid., p. 203.
11. Ibid., p. 21.
12. Ibid., p. 17.
13. Brooke, pp. 152–3.
14. Watson, pp. 247–8.
15. Plumb, pp. 127–30.
16. Hibbert, pp. 367–8.

## Chapter Nine

1. Livius, Book 1, paragraph 49, p. 58.
2. Ibid., Book 1, paragraphs 57–60, pp. 67–70.
3. Bokhanov, pp. 313–14.
4. Rose, pp. 211–18.
5. Bogdanor, pp. 1–2.

## Chapter Ten

1. Adamson, p. 100.
2. Milton, p. 42 (*Big Chief Elizabeth*).
3. Ibid., pp. 67–8.
4. Ibid., p. 68.
5. Weintraub, p. 353.

# Bibliography

Adamson, John (ed.), *The Princely Courts of Europe 1500–1750* (Weidenfeld & Nicolson, 1999)

Barber, Richard and Barker, Juliet, *Tournaments* (Boydell Press, 2000)

Bentley, Tom and Wilsdon, James (eds), *Monarchies: What are Kings and Queens For?* (Demos Paperback, 2002)

Black, J.B., *The Reign of Elizabeth 1558–1603* (Oxford History of England, Clarendon Press, 2nd edn, 1959)

Bokhanov, Alexander *et al.*, *The Romanovs: Love, Power and Tragedy* (Leppi Publications, 1993)

Bogdanor, Vernon, *The Monarchy and the Constitution* (Oxford University Press, 1997)

Bossuet, Jacques-Bénigne, *Politics Drawn from the Words of Holy Scripture* (Cambridge University Press, 1999)

Brooke, John, *King George III* (Panther Books, Granada Publishing, 1974)

Church, William, *Richelieu and Reasons of State* (Princeton University Press, 1972)

Clark, Sir George, *The Later Stuarts 1660–1714* (Oxford History of England, Clarendon Press, 1992)

Davies, Godfrey, *The Early Stuarts 1603–1660* (Oxford History of England, Clarendon Press, 2nd edn, 1959)

Einhard (trans. Samuel Epes Turner), *The Life of Charlemagne* (New York: Harper & Brothers, 1880, University of Michigan Press, 1960 reprint)

Erlanger, Philippe, *Louis XIV* (Weidenfeld & Nicolson, 1970)

Frazer, Sir James, *Lectures on the Early History of Kingship* (Macmillan, 1905)

——, *The Golden Bough* (Oxford World Classics, 1994)

Hatton, Ragnhild, *George I: Elector and King* (Thames & Hudson, 1978)

Hibbert, Christopher, *Queen Victoria, a Personal History* (HarperCollins, 2000)

James, Lawrence, *Raj: The Making and Unmaking of British India* (Little Brown & Co., 1997)

Kautilya (trans. R. Shamasastry), *Arthashastra* (Mysore: Wesleyan Mission Press, 1923)

Kershaw, Roger, *Monarchy in South East Asia: The Faces of Tradition in Transition* (Routledge, 2001)

# Bibliography

Lander, J.R., *The Limitations of English Monarchy in the Later Middle Ages* (The 1986 Joann Goodman Lectures, University of Toronto Press, 1989)

Lewis, Brenda Ralph, *The Aztecs* (Sutton Publishing, 1999)

——, *Ritual Sacrifice: A Concise History* (Sutton Publishing, 2001)

Livius, Titus (Livy), *The Rise of Rome*, Books 1–5 (Oxford World Classics, 1998)

Major, J. Russell, *From Renaissance Monarchy to Absolute Monarchy: French Kings, Nobles and Estates* (Johns Hopkins University Press, 1997)

Masanori, Nakamura, *The Japanese Monarchy: Ambassador Joseph Grew and the Making of the Symbol Emperor System 1931–1991* (M.E. Sharpe, 1992)

Mazumdar, Keshab Chandra, *Imperial Agra of the Moghuls* (Gaya Prasad & Sons, 1946)

Milton, Giles, *Big Chief Elizabeth* (Hodder & Stoughton, 2001)

——, *Samurai William: The Adventurer who Unlocked Japan* (Hodder & Stoughton, 2002)

Monod, Paul Kleber, *The Power of Kings: Monarchy and Religion in Europe 1589–1715* (Yale University Press, 1999)

Nicolson, Harold, *Monarchy* (Weidenfeld & Nicolson, 1962)

Packard, Jerrold M., *Sons of Heaven: A Portrait of the Japanese Monarchy* (Collier Books, Macmillan, 1989)

Paludan, Ann, *Chronicle of the Chinese Emperors* (Thames & Hudson, 1998)

Plumb, J.H., *The First Four Georges* (Classic History, Penguin Books, 1956)

Price, Roger, *The Revolutions of 1848* (Studies in European History: Humanities Press International, 1988)

Richardson, Glenn, *Renaissance Monarchy* (Arnold Publishers and Oxford University Press, 2002)

Rose, Kenneth, *King George V* (Weidenfeld & Nicolson, 1983)

Watson, J. Steven, *The Reign of George III 1770–1815* (Clarendon Press, 1992)

Weintraub, Stanley, *The Importance of Being Edward: King in Waiting 1841–1901* (John Murray, 2000)

Williams, Basil, *The Whig Supremacy 1714–1760* (The Oxford History of England, Clarendon Press, 1962)

Wood, Dorothy, *Leo VI's Concept of Divine Monarchy* (Monarchist Press Association, Historical Series No. 1, 1964)

Ziegler, Philip, *King Edward VIII* (Sutton Publishing, 2001)

# Index

# Index

# Index

# Index

# Index

# Index